CW01213046

THE ROYAL UNION

DIVINE ROYALTY

BARBARA ANN MARY MACK

authorHOUSE

AuthorHouse™
1663 Liberty Drive
Bloomington, IN 47403
www.authorhouse.com
Phone: 833-262-8899

© 2024 Barbara Ann Mary Mack. All rights reserved.

No part of this book may be reproduced, stored in a retrieval system, or transmitted by any means without the written permission of the author.

Published by AuthorHouse 11/15/2024

ISBN: 979-8-8230-3816-4 (sc)
ISBN: 979-8-8230-3815-7 (hc)
ISBN: 979-8-8230-3814-0 (e)

Library of Congress Control Number: 2024924917

Print information available on the last page.

Any people depicted in stock imagery provided by Getty Images are models, and such images are being used for illustrative purposes only. Certain stock imagery © Getty Images.

This book is printed on acid-free paper.

Because of the dynamic nature of the Internet, any web addresses or links contained in this book may have changed since publication and may no longer be valid. The views expressed in this work are solely those of the author and do not necessarily reflect the views of the publisher, and the publisher hereby disclaims any responsibility for them.

BEHOLD MY PRESENT TESTAMENT: THE CONTINUANCE OF MY OLD AND NEW TESTAMENTS, SAYS THE LORD GOD

THE ROYAL UNION

SUBTITLE

DIVINE ROYALTY

BY:

BARBARA ANN MARY MACK

BEGAN: OCTOBER 29, 2024

COMPLETED: NOVEMBER 10, 2024

CONTENTS

DEDICATION IX
ACKNOWLEDGMENT XI
INTRODUCTION.. XIII
BOOK 1-THE ROYAL UNION... XV
BOOK 2-LOVE IS HERE 19
BOOK 3-THE DANCE: THE HOLY DANCE 29
BOOK 4-WE'VE GOT A GOOD THING 43
BOOK 5-JOY 53
BOOK 6-IF ONLY YOU KNEW...................................... 79
BOOK 7-GOD'S HOLY STARS AND ME 97
BOOK 8-REALITY: SWEET, SWEET, REALITY 111
BOOK 9-THE URGENCY 127
BOOK 10-SALVATION 139
BOOK 11-MY TREASURE 155
BOOK 12-YOURS 167
BOOK 13-AMAZING IS HE 181
BOOK 14-A STRONG LOVE 193
BOOK 15-SOMEONE TO LOVE ME 201
BOOK 16-CHAINED AND BOUND............................ 211
BOOK 17-CLOSER TO ME 225
BOOK 18-A LIFE TIME WITH YOU 233

SOME OF MY OTHER GOD INSPIRED
PUBLISHED BOOKS..245

DEDICATION

TO THE DIVINE ROYAL ONES

ACKNOWLEDGMENT

THE PRESENCE OF THE DIVINE ROYAL ONES TRULY EXISTS, SAYS THE LORD GOD

INTRODUCTION

IN THE BEGINNING DIVINE LOVE EXITED HEAVEN'S SWEET OPEN GATES AND ENTERED THE BEINGS OF CHRIST JESUS, THE FATHER'S ONLY BEGOTTEN SON, AND BARBARA, THE FATHER'S CHOSEN DAUGHTER AND MESSENGER; GOD, THE FATHER'S ROYAL ONES. THE DIVINE ROYALS ONES ARE UNITED WITH GOD, THE HOLY TRINITY, FOR THEY ARE ALL IN AGREEMENT WITH EACH OTHER.

DIVINE LOVE MOVES IN THE MIDST OF THE ROYAL ONES; AND THEY HAVE SHARED THEIR UNION OF DIVINE LOVE WITH HEAVEN AND EARTH. LET ALL GIVE PRAISE TO ALMIGHTY GOD, THE ROYAL FATHER. FOR HE IS THE DIVINE ORCHESTRATOR AND ORIGIN OF ALL THAT IS GOOD AND HOLY.

LET THE UNENDING REALM OF LOVE BEGIN WITH GOD, THE FATHER, AS OUR HOLY GUIDE.

HALLELUJAH!!!

BOOK # ONE

THE ROYAL UNION

DIVINE ROYALTY MOVES IN THE MIDST OF EXISTENCE TODAY. LET US GIVE ALMIGHTY GOD, THE ETERNAL FATHER, CONTINUOUS PRAISE, GLORY, AND HONOR

BARBARA SPEAKING

DIVINE ROYALTY-
ORIGINATED FROM GOD, THE HEAVENLY **FATHER, ALMIGHTY.**

DIVINE ROYALTY MOVES IN **OUR MIDST TODAY-**
COME, DEAR ONES! LET US LISTEN TO WHAT **HE HAS TO SAY.**

FOR, ALMIGHTY **GOD, THE FATHER-**
NOW, INTRODUCES THE BLESSED WORLD TO CHRIST JESUS, AND BARBARA ANN MARY MACK, **HIS ROYAL BRIDE AND MESSENGER.**

LET US ALL **REJOICE, YOU SEE!**
FOR, WE ARE IN THE PRESENCE OF THE FATHER'S CHOICE OF **DIVINE ROYALTY!!!**

FOR, HOLY AND **TRUE, YOU SEE-**
ARE THE HEAVEN SENT WRITINGS THAT ARE **GIVEN TO ME.**

I WILL BOW MY **OBEDIENT ESSENCE-**
IN ALMIGHTY GOD, THE **FATHER'S, ROYAL PRESENCE.**

FOR, **HOLY, YOU SEE-**
IS THE GOD AND FATHER WHO HAS **CHOSEN BLESSED ME.**

HE HAS BLESSED HIS EARTHLY **LOVED ONES AND ME-**
IN THE ROYAL PRESENCE OF CHRIST **JESUS, THE ALMIGHTY.**

FOR, **HOLY AND TRUE-**
IS THE ROYAL GOD AND FATHER WHO HAS **INVITED ME AND YOU.**

HOLY, HOLY, HOLY-
IS OUR GOD AND FATHER'S POSITION AND ROYALTY.

BARBARA SPEAKING

Barbara Ann Mary Mack

DIVINE ROYALTY-
HAS REVEALED THE WELCOMED PRESENCE OF **GOD ALMIGHTY.**

FOR, HE IS THE **HOLY ROYAL ONE.**
HE IS GOD, THE FATHER'S, FAITHFUL AND **OBEDIENT BEGOTTEN SON.**

HE, CHRIST JESUS, IS **THE DIVINE LOVE-**
THAT REIGNS ON EARTH, AND IN **SWEET HEAVEN ABOVE.**

HE IS THE GENTLE LIFE-**SAVING LAMB, YOU SEE-**
WHO HAS UNITED HIS BLESSED HOLY SPIRIT **WITH HUMBLED ME.**

FOR, OUR **UNION, YOU SEE-**
SITS IN THE MIDST OF **DIVINE ROYALTY.**

HOLY, HOLY, HOLY-
IS THE ROYAL UNION OF BARBARA AND CHRIST JESUS; GOD, THE ROYAL SON, ALMIGHTY!!!

FOR, HE HAS CALLED **INTO EXISTENCE-**
HIS DIVINITY AND **ROYAL PRESENCE.**

HOLY AND TRUE-
IS THE GOD ORDERED UNION THAT **SEES ME THROUGH.**

OUR DIVINE UNION **IS GRACIOUS-**
FOR, IT IS A UNION THAT WAS CALLED INTO EXISTENCE BY **THE ROYAL POSITION OF CHRIST JESUS.**

THE ROYAL HOLY UNITED ONES (CHRIST JESUS AND BARBARA) HAVE ENTERED HEAVEN'S OPEN GATES

THE ROYAL UNITED ONES HAVE ENTERED **HEAVEN'S SWEET OPEN GATES.**
THE ROYAL COUPLE WILL NOT PERMIT **ANYTHING THAT HATES.**

FOR, **HOLY AND PURE-**
IS THE COUPLE THAT ALMIGHTY GOD AND HEAVEN'S RESIDENTS **TRULY ADORE.**

FOR, CHRIST JESUS, THE **FOREVER-LIVING KING-**
HAS INVITED HIS CHOSEN GUESTS TO GET A GLIMPSE OF THIS **HOLY AND ROYAL THING.**

FOR, **BARBARA, YOU SEE-**
IS THE ROYAL GIFT THAT CAME FROM **GOD, THE FATHER, ALMIGHTY.**

HOLY, YOU SEE-
IS THE ROYAL UNION OF BARBARA AND **CHRIST, THE ALMIGHTY.**

FOR, THE MULTITUDE OF GUESTS HAVE **ARRIVED, YOU SEE-**
AND NOW, THEY WILL LOOK UPON THE **DIVINE AND ROYAL UNITY.**

FOR, CHRIST, THE **ROYAL HOLY KING-**
HAS GIVEN BARBARA **HIS ROYAL RING.**

THE DIVINE **MUSIC PLAYS-**
AS THE INVITED GUESTS LISTEN TO EVERY WORD THAT THE DIVINE **ROYAL KING JESUS SAYS.**

THE HOLY MUSIC IS **SOFT AND LOW-**
AND THE CHOIR SINGS THE SACRED SONGS AS THE BEAUTY OF THE FATHER'S FACE AND **MIGHTY THRONE GLOW.**

THE ROYAL DANCE **HAS BEGUN-**
IN THE MIDST OF THE GRACE THAT SURROUNDS **GOD, THE FATHER'S, ROYAL SON.**

OH, SUCH **DIVINE GRACE-**
THAT SHINES ON THE ROYAL COUPLE'S **GLOWING UNITED FACE.**

FOR, **HOLY, YOU SEE-**
IS THE ROYAL KING WHO DANCES WITH **BLESSED ME.**

The Royal Union

LET ALL MOVE IN THE MIDST OF **DIVINE ROYALTY-**
FOR, WE ARE IN THE HOLY PRESENCE OF **GOD, THE FATHER, ALMIGHTY.**

LET ALL OF THE INVITED GUESTS **BOW, YOU SEE-**
FOR, WE ARE IN THE HOLY AND ROYAL PRESENCE OF **GOD, THE FATHER, ALMIGHTY.**

LET THE HOLY **KING SPEAK-**
LET HIM REVEAL THE ROYAL PLANS THAT **HE WILL SEEK.**

FOR, HIS HOLY **PLAN, YOU SEE-**
IS TO GIVE DIVINE PEACE TO THE LOVED ONES WHO ARE **CHOSEN BY HE.**

HOLY, HOLY, HOLY-
ARE THE ROYAL PLANS OF CHRIST JESUS, THE ALMIGHTY!!!

NO UNINVITED **GUEST, YOU SEE-**
WILL INTERRUPT NOR DISTURB THE ROYAL CELEBRATION OF **BARBARA AND CHRIST JESUS, THE ROYAL ALMIGHTY.**

NO UNINVITED **SPIRIT, YOU SEE-**
WILL ENTER THE GATES THAT LEAD TO THE HEAVENLY HOME OF **GOD ALMIGHTY.**

HOLY, HOLY, HOLY-
IS THE UNENDING REALM OF PEACE AND JOY THAT SURROUND THE HOME OF THE ROYAL ALMIGHTY.

IN THE MIDST OF THE ROYAL KING'S GREAT CELEBRATION

IN THE MIDST OF THE ROYAL **KING'S CELEBRATION-** ALMIGHTY GOD WILL REJOICE IN THE SOUND OF PRAISE THAT COMES FROM **THOSE OF EVERY NATION.**

HOLY, HOLY, HOLY-
IS THE GREAT AND JOYFUL CELEBRATION IN THE MIDST OF THE HEAVENLY HOME OF THE ROYAL KING ALMIGHTY!!!

HOLY, HOLY, HOLY-
IS THE ROYAL KING ALMIGHTY!!!

HOLINESS SURROUNDS THE ROYAL COUPLE

HOLINESS SURROUNDS THE ROYAL COUPLE AS THEY BOW IN FRONT OF **GOD, THE FATHER'S, MIGHTY THRONE ON HIGH.**
HOLINESS SURROUNDS THE LOVE AND UNION THAT **NO ONE CAN DENY.**

DIVINE RADIANCE-
SURROUNDS THE DIVINE ROYAL COUPLE AS THEY COMPLETE THEIR **HEAVENLY DANCE.**

FOR, **HOLY, YOU SEE-**
IS THE ROYAL COUPLE WHO REPRESENTS THE LIVING GOD, THE **FATHER'S, REALM OF SWEET REALITY.**

HOLY, HOLY, HOLY-
IS THE ROYAL COUPLE, WHICH INCLUDES BLESSED BARBARA AND KING JESUS, THE ALMIGHTY!!!

HOLY, HOLY, HOLY-
IS BARBARA, THE OBEDIENT BRIDE OF CHRIST ALMIGHTY!!!

FOR, **HER HOLINESS-**
REVEALS GOD, THE FATHER'S, ETERNAL REALM OF **DIVINE GOODNESS.**

HOLINESS AND DIVINE GRACE

HOLINESS AND **DIVINE GRACE-**
SHINES ON THE ROYAL COUPLE'S **UNITED FACE.**

FOR, THEY ARE ENVELOPED **IN THE GLORY-**
THAT REVEALS GOD, THE FATHER'S, **HOLY UNTOLD STORY.**

THEIR **APPEARANCE-**
SHINES IN THE HEAVENLY FATHER'S BLESSED AND **BELOVED PRESENCE.**

FOR, **HOLY, YOU SEE-**
IS THE COUPLE'S **DIVINE ROYALTY.**

THE IGNITED COUPLE **BOWS, YOU SEE-**
BEFORE THE SACRED THRONE OF **THE FATHER ALMIGHTY.**

THEIR **HEAVENLY GLOW-**
TRAVELS WHEREVER THE **BOTH OF THEM GO.**

HOLY AND REAL-
ARE THE BLESSINGS THAT THEY **RECEIVE AND FEEL.**

THE ROYAL COUPLE'S MOVEMENTS ARE **ELEGANT AND GRACEFUL-**
AS THEY FLOW IN THE PRESENCE OF THE GOD AND FATHER WHO IS **TRULY WONDERFUL.**

HOLY, HOLY, HOLY-
IS THE THRONE THAT HOLDS THE BEING OF GOD, THE **FATHER, ALMIGHTY!!!**

FOR, HE IS **SWEET DIVINITY-**

The Royal Union

WHO REIGNS IN THE MIDST OF **HEAVENLY ROYALTY.**

AND WHEN THE DIVINE ROYAL ONES UNITE WITH THE REALM OF JOY AND PEACE

AND WHEN THE DIVINE ROYAL ONES UNITE WITH **THE REALM OF JOY-**
THEY WILL EMBRACE THE REALM THAT SATAN **CANNOT DESTROY.**

WHEN THE ROYAL COUPLE UNITE WITH THE FATHER'S **REALM OF DIVINE PEACE-**
THEY WILL SHARE A LOVE THAT GOD, THE FATHER, **DOES RELEASE.**

FOR, **HOLY, YOU SEE-**
IS THE REALM OF DIVINITY THAT IS RELEASED BY **THE ROYAL FATHER, ALMIGHTY.**

THE INVITED GUESTS WILL RECEIVE THE HEAVENLY BLESSINGS THAT **THE ROYAL ONES RELEASE-**
AS THEY ENJOY THE FATHER'S REALM OF **DIVINE PEACE.**

FOR, THE **INVITED ONES-**
ARE GOD, THE FATHER'S, CHOSEN **DAUGHTERS AND SONS.**

HOLY, HOLY, HOLY-
ARE THE CHOSEN ONES WHO WILL ENJOY THE GREAT CELEBRATION THAT ACCOMPANIES THE COUPLE'S REALM OF DIVINE ROYALTY.

HOLY, HOLY, HOLY-
ARE THE DIVINE ROYAL ONES, BARBARA AND CHRIST JESUS, THE ALMIGHTY!!!

FOR, THEIR INDWELLING **HOLINESS**-
HAS COMFORTED AND SECURED GOD, THE FATHER'S, **REALM OF GOODNESS.**

HOLY, HOLY, HOLY-
IS CHRIST JESUS' LAND OF ROYALTY AND SWEET DIVINITY.

FOR, CHRIST, THE FOREVER-**LIVING ROYAL ONE**-
NOW REIGNS, AS GOD, THE FATHER'S, **TRIUMPHANT AND VICTORIOUS SON.**

HOLY, HOLY, HOLY, IS THE KING-
WHO REIGNS AND RULES IN THE MIDST OF HEAVEN AND EARTH'S BEAUTIFUL THING.

FOR, HE **RULES, YOU SEE**-
IN THE MIDST AND HOLY PRESENCE OF **GOD'S CHOSEN ONES AND ME.**

HOLY, HOLY, HOLY-
IS CHRIST JESUS, THE REALM OF DIVINE ROYALTY!!!

FOR, WE, THE UNITED ONES, ARE TRULY **BLESSED, YOU SEE-**
TO BE A WITNESS TO THE GREAT CELEBRATION, WHICH ANNOUNCES **THE DIVINE UNION OF HEAVENLY ROYALTY.**

HOLY, HOLY, HOLY-
IS THE ROYAL CELEBRATION THAT IS ORCHESTRATED AND DIRECTED BY GOD ALMIGHTY!!!

AND WE WERE ALL SEATED AROUND GOD, THE FATHER'S, MIGHTY ROYAL THRONE

AND WE, THE INVITED GUESTS, WERE ALL SEATED AROUND **THE DIVINE ROYAL KING'S MIGHTY THRONE ON HIGH-**
AND WE ALL SANG GLORIOUS SONGS OF PRAISE TO GOD, THE FATHER, AND CHRIST JESUS, HIS ONLY BEGOTTEN ROYAL SON, WHOM **WE WOULD NEVER ABANDON NOR DENY.**

FOR, HOLY AND **ETERNAL, YOU SEE-**
IS THE GOD AND ROYAL CHRIST JESUS, **THE INFINITE ALMIGHTY.**

HOLY, HOLY, HOLY-
IS THE ROYAL THRONE THAT HOLDS THE ETERNAL KING ALMIGHTY!!!

FOR, HE **SITS, YOU SEE**-
ON THE HOLY THRONE THAT WAS CALLED INTO EXISTENCE BY **GOD, THE ROYAL FATHER, ALMIGHTY.**

HOLY, HOLY, HOLY-
IS THE FATHER'S ONLY BEGOTTEN SON, CHRIST JESUS; THE ROYAL ALMIGHTY!!!

AND THE INVITED GUESTS HAVE QUIETED DOWN

THE GUESTS HAVE **QUIETED DOWN**-
FOR, THEY NOTICED THAT THE **ROYAL ONES WERE AROUND.**

THEY HAVE BEEN SEATED, AND HAVE **CALMED DOWN**-
FOR, CHRIST JESUS, THE ROYAL ONE, IS ABOUT TO UTTER **AN UNHEARD OF SOUND.**

FOR, HE **SPEAKS, YOU SEE**-
IN WORDS AND SOUNDS THAT ARE ONLY **FAMILIAR TO DIVINE ROYALTY**

HOLY, HOLY, HOLY-

ARE THE SOUNDS THAT EXIT THE BEING OF CHRIST JESUS, THE ALMIGHTY!!!

THE SOUNDS CAN BE **HEARD, YOU SEE-**
BY THOSE OF THE **DIVINE ROYAL FAMILY.**

FOR, HOLY, **TRUE, AND REAL-**
ARE THE UTTERED SOUNDS THAT THE DIVINE ROYAL ONES **CAN TRULY HEAR AND FEEL.**

HOLY, HOLY, HOLY-
ARE THE UNHEARD SOUNDS THAT EXIT THE BEING OF THE ROYAL KING ALMIGHTY!!!

AND THE INVITED GUESTS WERE SEATED AT THE REQUEST OF THE ROYAL KING

THE INVITED GUESTS WERE **SEATED, YOU SEE-**
AT THE REQUEST OF THE **ROYAL KING ALMIGHTY.**

WHAT THEY BEHELD **NEXT, YOU SEE-**
WAS SOMETHING THAT REVEALED THE TRUTH ABOUT THE **ROYAL SON'S TRUE IDENTITY.**

FOR, CHRIST **JESUS, YOU SEE-**
IS THE SON OF THE ORIGIN OF **DIVINE ROYALTY.**

AND, THE INVITED GUESTS, WERE PLEASED AND **MOVED, YOU SEE-**

Barbara Ann Mary Mack

TO LEARN OF THE FATHER'S ONLY BEGOTTEN **SON'S TRUE IDENTITY.**

HOLY, HOLY, HOLY-
IS THE ANNOUNCEMENT THAT REVEALED KING JESUS' **TRUE IDENTITY.**

FOR, WITH **GREAT REVERENCE-**
THE INVITED GUESTS BOWED IN THE **ROYAL ONE'S HOLY PRESENCE.**

FOR, CHRIST **JESUS, YOU SEE-**
IS THE ONLY BEGOTTEN SON OF **DIVINE ROYALTY.**

HOLY, HOLY, HOLY-
IS THE REALM OF ENDLESS HEAVEN MADE **ROYALTY!!!**

AND THE REMAINING GUESTS DID PAY HOMAGE TO THE ROYAL ONES

THE REMAINING GUESTS PAID **HOMAGE, YOU SEE-**
FOR, THEY WERE TOLD THAT THEY WERE IN THE HOLY PRESENCE OF **HEAVEN CALLED ROYALTY.**

HOLY, HOLY, HOLY-
IS CHRIST JESUS, THE ROYAL KING ALMIGHTY!!!

DIVINE ROYALTY HAS ENTERED THE DINING AREA

DIVINE ROYALTY-
HAS ENTERED THE DINING AREA, WHICH HOLDS THE INVITED **GUESTS OF GOD ALMIGHTY.**

DIVINE ROYALTY HAS ENTERED THE DINING AREA **IN SWEET HEAVEN.**
HE IS ACCOMPANIED BY HIS INVITED GUESTS AND **FAITHFUL CHILDREN.**

HE IS SEATED AT **HIS OVAL TABLE-**
WITH THOSE WHO ARE **SPIRITUALLY ABLE.**

THE ROYAL MEAL IS **SERVED, YOU SEE-**
IN THE DIVINE PRESENCE OF **JEHOVAH GOD, THE FATHER, ALMIGHTY.**

THE DIVINE MEAL IS **SERVED, YOU SEE-**
IN THE HOLY PRESENCE OF **THE ROYAL TRINITY.**

FOR, HOLY AND **TRUE, YOU SEE-**
IS THE MEAL THAT WAS PREPARED BY **GOD, THE FATHER, ALMIGHTY.**

THE DIVINE MEAL WAS **FILLING AND SWEET-**
IT IS CONSIDERED **A ROYAL AND HEAVENLY TREAT.**

Barbara Ann Mary Mack

HOLY, HOLY, HOLY-
IS THE MEAL THAT WAS PREPARED AND SERVED BY THE ROYAL HANDS OF GOD, THE FATHER, ALMIGHTY!!!

FOR, HOLY AND **TRUE, YOU SEE**-
WAS THE MEAL THAT WAS SERVED TO **THE ROYAL KING AND ME.**

HOLY, HOLY, HOLY-
IS THE SERVITUDE OF GOD, THE FATHER, ALMIGHTY!!!

PEACE, DIVINE PEACE, FLOWS THROUGH THE GREAT ROYAL CELEBRATION

DIVINE PEACE FLOWS THROUGH THE ROOMS OF **THE GREAT DIVINE ROYAL CELEBRATION.**
FOR, THERE IS NOTHING BUT DIVINE PEACE THAT SPEAKS TO THE INVITED GUESTS FROM **EVERY BLESSED NATION.**

FOR, **DIVINE ROYALTY**-
HAS INTERVENE IN THE MIDST OF THE GUESTS WHO WERE INVITED BY **THE ROYAL GOD AND KING ALMIGHTY.**

FOR, **HOLY AND TRUE**-
IS THE GOD WHO HAS **INVITED ALL OF YOU.**

The Royal Union

BOOK # TWO

LOVE IS HERE

LOVE IS HERE

SUBTITLE:

LET US REJOICE!!!

BY:

BARBARA ANN MARY MACK

BEGAN: NOVEMBER 1, 2024

COMPLETED: NOVEMBER 2, 2024

INTRODUCTION TO DIVINE UNENDING LOVE

LOVE IS HERE

BARBARA SPEAKING

LOVE IS TRULY HERE-
FOR, WE WERE CREATED BY A HOLY GOD WHO **DOES CARE.**

DIVINE LOVE IS **ALWAYS IN OUR MIDST**-
FOR, WE SERVE A MIGHT WHO **DOES EXIST.**

HE IS VISIBLE TO **THOSE WHO BELIEVE**-
FOR, WE ARE CONSTANTLY SHOWERED WITH THE DAILY BLESSINGS AND **DIVINE PROMISES THAT WE RECEIVE.**

WE **TRULY ADORE**-
THE HOLY ONE WHO HAS OPENED **EVERY BLESSED DOOR.**

FOR, WE ARE ENCOMPASSED **WITH THE LOVE**-
THAT IS RELEASED BY OUR HOLY GOD IN **SWEET HEAVEN ABOVE.**

FOR, **HOLY AND TRUE-**
IS THE LOVE THAT OUR HOLY GOD DESCENDS EVERY DAY TO **BELOVED ME AND YOU.**

MY MIND, BODY, AND SOUL **WILL EMBRACE-**
ALMIGHTY GOD'S HOLY HEAVENLY SPIRITUALLY **GLOWING FACE.**

FOR, MY BLESSED SPIRIT CAN **TRULY FEEL-**
THE LOVE OF THE ONLY GOD WHO IS **ETERNAL AND REAL.**

HOLY, HOLY, HOLY-
IS THE UNENDING REALM OF DIVINE LOVE THAT IS RELEASED BY ALMIGHTY GOD, TO THE EARTHLY CHILDREN OF CHRIST JESUS, THE ALMIGHTY!!!

I LONG **TO SHARE-**
THE UNCONDITIONAL AND UNENDING LOVE, AND FRIEND, WHO IS **ALWAYS NEAR.**

I LONG **TO SHARE-**
THE LOVE AND FRIENDSHIP THAT I RECEIVE EVERY DAY FROM **THE CREATOR AND GOD WHO DOES CARE.**

I WILL SHARE MY DIVINE KNOWLEDGE WITH **EVERYONE WHOM I GREET.**

I WILL SHARE THIS GOOD NEWS WITH EVERYONE WHOM **MY BLESSED SOUL AND BODY MEET.**

I WILL SHARE WITH THE **UNKNOWN STRANGER-** THE LOVE THAT DESCENDS TO US FROM GOD, OUR ORIGIN, **AND HEAVENLY FATHER.**

I WILL SHARE WITH **MY BLESSED FAMILY-** THE DAILY LOVE THAT I TRUST AND **RECEIVE FROM GOD ALMIGHTY.**

I WILL SHARE CHRIST **JESUS' GIFT OF LIFE-** THAT IS OFFERED TO THE BELIEVING **HUSBAND AND WIFE.**

I WILL **PROCLAIM-** THE HOLINESS OF CHRIST **JESUS' BLESSED NAME.**

HOLY IS THE ETERNAL **NAME OF CHRIST JESUS-** FOR, HE IS THE DESCENDED GOD WHO MOVES IN THE **MIDST OF BLESSED US.**

HOLY, HOLY, HOLY- **IS THE HEAVEN SENT GIFT OF LOVE CALLED CHRIST ALMIGHTY!!!**

HE IS THE GIFT OF DIVINE LOVE THAT **EXITED HEAVEN'S SWEET OPEN GATES.**

HE IS THE LOVE THAT **THE NEEDY WORLD WAITS.**

HE IS THE LOVELY ROAD THAT **LEADS TO ETERNAL LIFE-**
HE IS THE LOVE THAT **REMOVES WORLDLY STRIFE.**

HOLY, HOLY, HOLY-
IS THE FATHER'S GIFT OF LOVE CALLED CHRIST ALMIGHTY!!!

HIS REALM OF LOVE MOVES IN THE MIDST OF **EARTH'S NEEDY RESIDENTS TODAY-**
AS HIS MESSENGERS LEAD HIS EARTHLY FLOCK TO **HIS LIFE REWARDING HOLY WAY.**

HIS LOVE IS THE DIVINE REALM OF **TRUTH, YOU SEE-**
THAT GUIDES THE CHILDREN WHO BELIEVE IN **THE FOREVER-LIVING CHRIST ALMIGHTY.**

LOVE EXISTS. LOVE EXISTS. **DIVINE LOVE DOES EXIST-**
FOR, HE MOVES EVERY DAY, **WITHIN OUR BLESSED MIDST.**

HOLY IS CHRIST JESUS, **THE FATHER'S GIFT OF LOVE-**
FOR, HE DESCENDED TO US FROM **SWEET HEAVEN ABOVE.**

HE IS THE **LINK, YOU SEE-**
THAT CONNECTS THE SOULS THAT **BELONG TO YOU AND ME.**

LOVE IS HERE, LOVE IS HERE; **LOVE IS TRULY HERE.**
FOR, CHRIST JESUS IS THE FATHER'S SENT LOVE THAT IS **VERY, VERY NEAR.**

HOLY IS THE **REALM OF LOVE-**
THAT ENTERED EARTH'S NEEDY PRESENCE FROM **SWEET HEAVEN ABOVE.**

I LOOK UP TO THE HEAVEN DESCENDED **LOVE EVERY DAY-**
AS I FOLLOW HIS LIFE **GIVING HOLY WAY.**

HOLY, HOLY, HOLY-
IS THE REALM OF UNENDING LOVE CALLED CHRIST JESUS, THE ALMIGHTY!!!

BOOK # THREE

THE DANCE: THE HOLY DANCE

THE DANCE: THE HOLY DANCE

BY:

BARBARA ANN MARY MACK

BEGAN: OCTOBER 29, 2024

COMPLETED: NOVEMBER 3, 2024

THE DIVINE ROYAL DANCE

BARBARA SPEAKING

DANCE! DANCE! DANCE!
FOR, THIS IS A ONCE IN A **LIFETIME HOLY CHANCE!**

BEHOLD **EVERYONE-**
THE DANCE THAT I SHARE WITH GOD, THE FATHER'S, **ONLY BEGOTTEN SON!**

BEHOLD THE HEAVEN **BOUND DANCE-**
THAT IS VISIBLE IN **JUST ONE GLANCE!**

FOR, GOD, **THE ALMIGHTY-**
HAS CHOSEN TO DANCE WITH **BLESSED ME.**

HOLY, HOLY, HOLY-
IS THE DANCE THAT I SHARE WITH THE BLESSED SPIRIT OF GOD ALMIGHTY!!!

I WILL DANCE IN THE MIDST OF SWEET **UNINTERRUPTED DIVINITY-**
AS MY SPIRIT INHALE THE HOLY PRESENCE OF ALMIGHTY GOD, **THE UNIFIED HOLY TRINITY.**

FOR, **HOLY, YOU SEE-**

IS THE DANCE THAT INCLUDES GOD, THE FATHER, **AND BLESSED ME.**

DANCE IN THE MIDST AND PRESENCE OF **DIVINE ROYALTY-**
AS YOU HOLD ON TO THE HAND OF **CHRIST JESUS, THE ALMIGHTY.**

MOVE WITH **DIVINE GRACE-**
AS YOU BEHOLD THE EXPRESSION THAT IS ON **GOD'S JOYFUL FACE.**

FOR, **HOLY, YOU SEE-**
IS THE BLESSED **DANCING TRINITY.**

FOR, GOD, THE **FATHER, YOU SEE-**
DANCES WITH THOSE WHO ARE **SPIRITUALLY WORTHY.**

HOLY, HOLY, HOLY-
IS THE DANCE OF BARBARA AND THE BLESSED TRINITY!!!

FOR, HE **MOVES, YOU SEE-**
TO THE SACRED BEAT AND MUSIC OF GOD'S HOLY ANGELS, CHOIRS, **AND HEAVENLY ROYALTY.**

MY BLESSED FEET-

MOVE TO THE **HEAVEN SENT BEAT.**

FOR, **HOLY, YOU SEE-**
IS THE MUSIC THAT DESCENDED WITH **CHRIST ALMIGHTY.**

MOVE, **O BLESSED FEET!**
MOVE TO THE SOUND OF GOD'S HOLY MELODIOUS TUNES AND **DRUMMERS BEAT!**

MOVE, MOVE, MOVE, **O BLESSED FEET OF MINE-**
AS YOU DANCE TO THE RHYTHM DURING THIS **PRAISE WORTHY TIME!**

MOVE, O BLESSED BODY-
FOR, YOU ARE DANCING AROUND HEAVEN'S MIGHTY THRONE IN **THE COMPANY OF GOD ALMIGHTY!!!**

SWAY, SWAY, SWAY-
SWAY IN THE MIDST OF GOD'S GLORY AS YOU ENJOY **HEAVEN'S UNENDING DAY!**

FOR, YOU NOW, **DANCE, YOU SEE-**
IN THE MIDST OF HEAVEN'S GREAT MULTITUDE AND **THE ANGELIC COMPANY.**

DANCE, O BLESSED BARBARA!

The Royal Union

SWING LEFT AND RIGHT WITH ALMIGHTY **GOD, YOUR HEAVENLY PARTNER!**

MOVE TO **THE HEAVENLY SOUND-**
THAT IS **ALWAYS AROUND.**

MOVE TO THE **RHYTHM AND BEAT-**
AS YOU MOVE YOUR **PRAISING HANDS AND FEET!**

THE SACRED DANCE IS VERY EXCLUSIVE

THE SACRED DANCE IS VERY **EXCLUSIVE, YOU SEE-**
FOR, IT IS A DANCE THAT WAS ORDERED FOR AND BY **ALMIGHTY GOD AND ME.**

IT IS A DANCE THAT IS **PURE AND HOLY-**
IT IS THE DANCE THAT IS ENJOYED BY **BARBARA AND THE BLESSED HOLY TRINITY.**

FOR, ALMIGHTY GOD, **THE FATHER, YOU SEE-**
HAS ORDERED THIS SACRED DANCE IN THE HOLY PRESENCE OF **HIS HEAVENLY COMPANY.**

FOR, **HOLY, YOU SEE-**
IS THE ATTENTION THAT IS GIVEN **TO BLESSED ME.**

BARBARA SPEAKING TO GOD, THE FATHER

I WILL MOVE TO YOUR HEAVENLY BEAT, **DEAR FATHER.**
FOR, I AM YOUR GRATEFUL AND **OBEDIENT DAUGHTER.**

I WILL TAKE YOUR GRAND **SPIRITUAL HAND-**
SO THAT MY INNER BEING WILL **FULLY UNDERSTAND.**

FOR, IT IS A **JOYFUL DELIGHT-**
TO HAVE THE BELOVED TRINITY WITHIN MY WORTHY **AND OBEDIENT SIGHT.**

FOR, **HOLY AND TRUE-**
IS THE LOVE THAT SEES MY **BLESSED SOUL THROUGH.**

BARBARA SPEAKING TO HER GRATEFUL HEART

MOVE, O BEATING GRATEFUL **HEART OF MINE-**
SHOW YOUR SINCERE GRATITUDE DURING THIS **BLESSED PERIOD OF TIME.**

BARBARA SPEAKING TO GOD ALMIGHTY

FOR, HOLY, **ETERNAL AND TRUE-**
IS THE UNINTERRUPTED LOVE THAT **COMES FROM YOU.**

FOR, YOUR UNENDING **REALM OF GRACE-**

The Royal Union

SHINES ON YOUR LOVELY **HEAVENLY FACE.**

HOLY, HOLY, HOLY-
IS THE HEAVENLY FACIAL GLOW OF GOD ALMIGHTY!!!

YOU HAVE **PROVEN-**
YOUR SACRED LOVE FOR ALL OF YOUR OBEDIENT AND **FAITHFUL CHILDREN.**

<u>**BARBARA SPEAKING**</u>

HOLY, HOLY, HOLY-
IS THE GRATITUDE OF GOD ALMIGHTY!!!

FOR, HE **MOVES, YOU SEE-**
TO THE HEAVENLY BEAT THAT EMITS FROM THE INSTRUMENTS THAT WERE **CALLED INTO EXISTENCE BY GOD, THE ALMIGHTY.**

MY BLESSED BODY MOVES TO **THE HEAVENLY BEAT-**
AS MY SPIRIT TAKES CONTROL OF **MY EXCITED ROYAL FEET.**

MY BLESSED **SPIRIT DANCES-**
IN ALMIGHTY GOD'S HOLY **REJOICING PRESENCE.**

FOR, THE HEAVENLY **BEAT, YOU SEE-**

HAS CAPTURED THE BLESSED SPIRITS OF **THE LORD GOD AND ME.**

LET OUR UNIFIED SPIRITS MOVE TO **THE JOYFUL RHYTHM-**
THAT FLOWS IN THE HOLY PRESENCE OF **GOD'S HEAVENLY CREATION.**

LET THE HEAVENLY **LANDS PRAISE-**
THEIR HOLY CREATOR THROUGHOUT **THESE HEAVENLY DAYS!**

FOR, SWEET **EXISTENCE, YOU SEE-**
DANCES WITH **ANIMATED ME.**

HOLY, HOLY, HOLY-
IS THE DANCE THAT MY BLESSED SPIRIT SHARES WITH CHRIST JESUS, THE ALMIGHTY!!!

<u>BARBARA SPEAKING TO CHRIST JESUS</u>

DANCE, O **BLESSED SAVIOR!**
DANCE IN THE HOLY PRESENCE OF ALMIGHTY **GOD, OUR REJOICING FATHER!**

FOR, **HE IS-**
PLEASED WITH THE SON (CHRIST JESUS) AND DAUGHTER (BARBARA) **THAT ARE HIS.**

The Royal Union

DANCE, LORD GOD!
DANCE WITH ME IN THE MIDST OF YOUR HOLY **ANGELS AND DIVINE LOVE!**

FOR YOU ARE **THE VICTORY-**
THAT IS THE FATHER'S REALM OF **SWEET INFINITY!**

YOU, **LORD JESUS-**
ARE THE LORD AND KING OVER THE FAITHFUL ONES **AND THE RIGHTEOUS.**

DANCE! DANCE! DANCE!
LET THE REJOICING MULTITUDE BEHOLD OUR HOLY MOVES IN **JUST ONE GLANCE!**

FOR, **HOLY, YOU SEE-**
IS THE DANCE THAT IS ORCHESTRATED BY **GOD, THE ALMIGHTY.**

DANCE! DANCE! DANCE!
LET US GIVE EARTH'S RESIDENTS AND THE BLESSED ONES **A GLORIOUS CHANCE!**

FOR, YOUR JUDGEMENT IS **FAIR AND HOLY-**
AND, YOU WANT WHAT IS GOOD AND JUST FOR **THE CHILDREN OF GOD ALMIGHTY.**

MOVE TO OUR **HEAVEN ORDERED BEAT!**

Barbara Ann Mary Mack

MOVE, LORD JESUS, MOVE! FOR, DANCING WITH YOUR HOLY SPIRIT IS **TRULY A DIVINE GIFT AND TREAT!**

FOR, **HOLY AND TRUE-**
IS THE MESSENGER (BARBARA) AND LIVING DAUGHTER WHO WERE **CHOSEN TO DANCE WITH LOVING YOU.**

HOLY, HOLY, HOLY-
IS MY DANCE WITH CHRIST ALMIGHTY!!!

AND THE HEAVENLY BEAT WILL LAST THROUGHOUT SWEET ETERNITY

THE HEAVENLY BEAT WILL LAST THROUGHOUT **SWEET ETERNITY-**
FOR, MY BLESSED SPIRIT HAS UNIFIED WITH OUR **ETERNAL GOD ALMIGHTY!!!**

SWEET ETERNITY-
HAS CALLED INTO EXISTENCE THE REJOICING TUNES THAT FLOW IN THE HOLY PRESENCE OF CHRIST JESUS, **THE FOREVER-LIVING GOD ALMIGHTY.**

HOLY, HOLY, HOLY-
ARE THE TUNES THAT SURROUND THE REJOICING **THRONE OF GOD ALMIGHTY!!**

AND THE HOLY SOUNDS OF OUR DANCE WILL DISSIPATE **THROUGHOUT SWEET ETERNITY.**
IN THE PRESENCE OF **DIVINE ROYALTY...**

ALLELUIA!!!

BOOK # FOUR

WE'VE GOT A GOOD THING

WE'VE GOT A GOOD THING

BY:

BARBARA ANN MARY MACK

BEGAN: OCTOBER 29, 2024

COMPLETED: NOVEMBER 4, 2024

A LOVE LIKE NO OTHER

BARBARA SPEAKING

A LOVE **LIKE NO OTHER**-
A LOVE THAT DESCENDED TO ME FROM ALMIGHTY GOD, **MY ETERNAL LOVE AND DIVINE HEAVENLY FATHER.**

IT'S **THE REAL THING**-
FOR, IT WAS GIVEN TO ME BY THE SACRED **GOD AND MIGHTY KING.**

HOLINESS IS **THE GOOD THING**-
THAT MAKES MY JOYFUL SOUL **DANCE AND SING.**

IT IS AN UNFORGETTABLE LOVE THAT MOVES IN **YOUR BLESSED MIDST.**
IT IS A DIVINE LOVE THAT IS NURTURED AND CARED FOR BY **THE ONLY GOD WHO DOES EXIST.**

IT IS A VERY **GOOD THINGS**-
FOR, IT IS FILLED WITH WONDERFUL HEAVENLY KNOWLEDGE AND **GOOD TIDINGS.**

IT IS FILLED WITH KNOWLEDGE PERTAINING TO CHRIST JESUS, THE HEAVENLY AND **EARTHLY KING OF KINGS.**
IT IS A LOVE THAT **MY HEART SINGS.**

OH, **THE GRATITUDE-**
THAT HAS JOINED CHRIST **JESUS' HEAVENLY MULTITUDE.**

FOR, I AM TRULY **GRATEFUL, YOU SEE-**
FOR THE MANY GOOD THINGS THAT GOD HAS GIVEN TO **MY LOVED ONES AND ME.**

I WILL SIT BACK AND **ENJOY, YOU SEE-**
THE MANY TREASURES AND GOOD THINGS THAT OUR LIVING SAVIOR AND GOD HAS GIVEN TO **THE BLESSED ONES AND ME.**

MY HEART AND SOUL **TINGLES, YOU SEE-**
AS I GAZE UPON THE GOOD THINGS THAT MY SAVING GOD HAS GIVEN TO HIS BLESSED FAITHFUL AND OBEDIENT CHILDREN **AND ME.**

HOLY, HOLY, HOLY-
ARE THE GOOD THINGS THAT COME FROM CHRIST JESUS, THE ALMIGHTY!!!

FOR, HOLY IS OUR RELATIONSHIP, **YOU SEE-**

GOODNESS SURROUNDS THE DIVINE LOVE THAT **HE HAS FOR ME.**

OH, HOW **GRAND IT IS-**
TO SHARE A DIVINE RELATIONSHIP THAT IS **MINE AND HIS.**

HOLY IS **OUR GOOD THING-**
FOR, MY MIND, BODY AND SOUL, ARE UNIFIED WITH MY **GOD AND HEAVENLY KING.**

OH, HOW **JOYFUL-**
TO BE IN A DIVINE RELATIONSHIP WITH SOMEONE WHO IS **GOOD, HOLY, AND WONDERFUL.**

FOR, HOLY, **YOU SEE-**
IS THE FRIENDSHIP THAT WAS CALLED INTO EXISTENCE **AND REALITY.**

FOR, MY HUMBLED SOUL **BOWS, YOU SEE-**
IN THE MIDST OF ALMIGHTY **GOD'S SWEET DIVINITY.**

FOR, HOLY IS **THE LAND-**
THAT WAS SAVED BY GOD'S **HOLY UNINTERRUPTED HAND.**

HE IS **MARVELOUS-**
HIS REALM OF EXISTENCE **IS GLORIOUS.**

The Royal Union

SHOUT! SHOUT! SHOUT! SHOUT WITH DIVINE GLADNESS, **ALL YOU LANDS!**
FOR, WE ARE IN THE POWER OF GOD'S **HOLY AND PURE HANDS!**

SHOUT! SHOUT! SHOUT!
LET THE LORD GOD AND I SHOW THE WORLD WHAT **OUR HOLY UNION IS ALL ABOUT!**

FOR, **HE IS WORTHY-**
TO RECEIVE OUR SHOUTS OF PRAISE AND **UNENDING GLORY.**

FOR, **HOLY AND TRUE-**
IS THE GOD WHO MOVES IN THE MIDST OF **ME AND YOU.**

NO UNION LIKE OUR DIVINE ROYAL UNION

<u>**BARBARA SPEAKING TO THE LORD GOD AND KING**</u>

MY LORD **GOD ABOVE-**
THERE'S NO UNION LIKE THE UNION THAT YOU AND **I HAVE AND LOVE.**

FOR, OUR **ROYAL UNION-**
RULES IN THE MIDST OF **OUR PERSONAL NATION.**

FOR, OUR **PERSONAL NATION-**

INCLUDES ONLY OUR GOD, THE **FATHER'S, ORDERED UNION.**

HOLY IS OUR **UNIFIED NATION.**
GLORIOUS IS THE UNION THAT HAS CAPTIVATED **YOUR BELIEVING CHILDREN.**

FOR, **HOLY, YOU SEE-**
IS THE LAND THAT HAS CAPTIVATED **OUR DIVINE UNITY.**

HOLY, HOLY, HOLY-
IS OUR REALM OF GOD ORDERED UNITY!!!

MY BLESSED SPIRIT WILL WALK WITH YOURS, MY ROYAL GOD AND FOREVER REIGNING KING

<u>**BARBARA SPEAKING TO THE ROYAL KING; CHRIST JESUS**</u>

I WILL WALK WITH YOU THROUGHOUT **EACH GLORIOUS DAY-**
SO THAT MY BLESSED MIND AND SOUL MAY CAPTURE **EVERY WORD THAT YOU SAY.**

FOR, WHEN YOUR HOLY SPIRIT **SPEAKS TO ME-**
MY BEING TREMBLES IN THE HOLY PRESENCE OF **GOD ALMIGHTY.**

The Royal Union

WAKE ME, O ROYAL GOD

BARBARA SPEAKING TO CHRIST JESUS, THE DIVINE ROYAL ONE

WAKE ME. WAKE ME. WAKE ME.
WAKE ME, O BLESSED REALM OF **DIVINE UNITY!**

WAKE ME-
IN THE HOLY PRESENCE OF MY **SAVING GOD ALMIGHTY.**

FOR, HOLY AND UNFORGETTABLE **IS THE BEING-**
WHO HAS UNITED ME WITH CHRIST JESUS, MY REALM OF UNITY; **AND MY HOLY GOD AND KING.**

I WILL TRAVEL THROUGH THE UNIVERSE IN THE PRESENCE OF MY **HOLY KING AND GOD.**
MY BLESSED SPIRIT WILL MOVE BY THE STRENGTH AND POWER OF **HIS DIVINE LOVE.**

FOR, **HOLY, YOU SEE-**
IS THE UNION THAT ALMIGHTY GOD SHARES **WITH OBEDIENT ME.**

HOLY, HOLY, HOLY-
IS THE ROYAL GOD ALMIGHTY!!!

BOOK # FIVE

JOY

JOY

SUBTITLE:

DIVINE HAPPINESS

BY:

BARBARA ANN MARY MACK

BEGAN: OCTOBER 29, 2024

COMPLETED: NOVEMBER 4, 2024

INTRODUCTION

JOY, JOY, HEAVENLY JOY

IN THE BEGINNING THE REALM OF DIVINE HAPPINESS MOVED THROUGH THE OPEN GATES THAT SURROUND THE ENTRANCE TO **SWEET HEAVEN, YOU SEE.**

IN THE BEGINNING, THE REALM OF JOY ACCOMPANIED THE ROYAL ONES AND **THE REALM OF SWEET DIVINITY.**

IN THE BEGINNING SPIRITUAL LIFE **EXISTED, YOU SEE-**
FOR, IN THE BEGINNING, THE REALM OF EXISTENCE WAS **CALLED GOD ALMIGHTY.**

IN THE BEGINNING THERE WERE SOUNDS, AND SOUNDS; AND MIGHTY SOUNDS THAT REVEALED THE LAUGHTER **AND JOY, YOU SEE-**
THAT PROCEED FROM THE BEINGS OF **THE SPIRITS OF DIVINE SWEET ROYALTY.**

FOR, IN THE **BEGINNING, YOU SEE-**
THE GATES OF SWEET HEAVEN SHELTERED **THE HOME OF DIVINE ROYALTY.**

THE REALMS OF **HEAVENLY JOY-**
EXHIBITED A LOVE THAT NO EVIL **SOURCE CAN DESTROY.**

IT IS A REALM OF **DIVINE HAPPINESS-**
THAT REVEALS THE **ROYAL ONES HOLINESS.**

FOR, **HOLY, YOU SEE-**
IS THE HAPPINESS THAT **SURROUNDS SWEET DIVINITY.**

LET THE OPEN GATES TO SWEET HEAVEN RISE IN THE MIDST OF **SWEET ROYALTY-**
AS ALMIGHTY GOD REVEALS HIS **SEA OF FLOWING DIVINITY.**

FOR, **HOLY, YOU SEE-**
IS THE REALM CALLED **GOD, THE ALMIGHTY.**

HOLY, HOLY, HOLY-
ARE THE ROYAL ONES AND THEIR REALM OF SWEET UNENDING DIVINITY!!!

LET THE REALM OF JOY AND **DIVINE HAPPINESS-**
REVEAL ITS REALITY IN THE MIDST OF GOD'S HOLY **PRESENCE AND GOODNESS.**

ALLELUIA! ALLELUIA! ALLELUIA!!!

REALMS AND REALMS OF SWEET HEAVEN SENT JOY

REALMS AND REALMS OF SWEET **HEAVEN SENT JOY**-
IT IS A DIVINE JOY THAT THE REALM OF DESTRUCTION **CAN NEVER DESTROY.**

IT IS A JOY THAT REVEALS GOD'S REALM **OF DIVINE PEACE-**
IT IS A HAPPINESS THAT THE GATES OF SWEET **HEAVEN DO RELEASE.**

IT IS A REALM THAT MY HEART **AND SOUL LONG FOR.**
IT IS THE ENTRANCE TO **CHRIST JESUS' OPEN DOOR.**

OH, HOW **GRAND IT IS-**
TO EXPERIENCE **THE JOY THAT IS HIS.**

FOR, ALMIGHTY **GOD, YOU SEE-**
GIVES THE DIVINE JOY THAT **SATISFIES BLESSED ME.**

HE IS MY JOY THAT KEEPS ME **THROUGHOUT EACH DAY-**
HE IS THE SATISFACTION THAT GUIDES ME TO HIS HOLY **LIFE REWARDING WAY.**

HE IS **THE ALMIGHTY-**
HE IS THE HOLY ORIGIN OF **SWEET ROYALTY.**

HE IS THE FORETOLD GOOD **SHEPHERD, YOU SEE-**
WHO WATCHES OVER **BLESSED YOU AND ME.**

HE IS THE HOLY REALM THAT PRODUCES AND RELEASES **DIVINE JOY AND HAPPINESS-**
HE IS ALMIGHTY GOD, THE REALM OF **UNENDING HOLINESS.**

HE IS THE ETERNAL **ROYAL GOD, YOU SEE-**
FOR, HE IS THE LIFE THAT PRODUCED THE GLORIOUS THINGS THAT ARE GIVEN TO **MY BLESSED LOVED ONES AND ME.**

ROYALTY, DIVINE ROYALTY-
FOLLOWS THE REALM OF **SWEET DIVINITY.**

HOLY, HOLY, HOLY-
IS OUR ROYAL GOD ALMIGHTY!!!

FOR, HIS HOLINESS **SUSTAINS US-**
AS WE ENJOY THE ROYAL PRESENCE OF **THE FOREVER-LIVING CHRIST JESUS.**

HOLY, HOLY, HOLY-
IS THE EXISTING ROYAL CHRIST ALMIGHTY!!!

Barbara Ann Mary Mack

FOR, **HOLY AND TRUE-**
IS THE HEAVENLY JOY THAT **SEES ME THROUGH.**

I WILL AWAKE IN THE MIDST OF **SWEET UNENDING DIVINITY-**
AS I CLING TO THE JOY THAT IS **RELEASED BY CHRIST ALMIGHTY.**

FOR, **HOLY, YOU SEE-**
IS THE REALM OF HEAVENLY JOY THAT IS RELEASED BY ALMIGHTY GOD **FOR BLESSED ME.**

JOY! JOY! I WILL CLING TO THE REALM OF UNENDING DIVINE JOY!!!

BARBARA SPEAKING

JOY! JOY! THE REALM OF UNENDING **JOY, YOU SEE-**
HAS CAPTURED THE BLESSED **DAUGHTER OF GOD ALMIGHTY!**

FOR HIS REALM OF UNENDING **DIVINE JOY, YOU SEE-**
MOVES EVERY DAY **WITH BLESSED ME.**

BARBARA SPEAKING TO GOD'S REALM OF DIVINE JOY

MOVE WITH ME, O GREAT AND **HOLY REALM OF JOY-**

The Royal Union

AS I CLING TO MY HOLY HEAVENLY GOD. FOR HE WATCHES OVER **THE SLEEPING LITTLE GIRL AND BOY.**

LET **ALL OF US-**
REJOICE IN THE ROYAL AND HOLY PRESENCE OF **THE FOREVER-LIVING CHRIST JESUS.**

FOR, HIS HOLY UNINTERRUPTED **GOODNESS, YOU SEE-** TAKES VERY GOOD CARE OF **HIS EARTHLY LOVED ONES AND ME.**

HOLY, HOLY, HOLY-
IS THE GIFT OF JOY THAT COMES FROM OUR HEAVENLY GENEROUS FATHER AND GOD ALMIGHTY!!!

FOR, HIS **REALM OF DIVINE SWEETNESS-**
GIVES COMFORT TO HIS LOVED ONES, AS WE ENJOY AND EXPERIENCE **HIS HEAVEN SENT GOODNESS.**

HOLY, HOLY, HOLY-
IS THE REALM OF JOY THAT IS CALLED GOD ALMIGHTY!!!

HOLY, HOLY, HOLY-
IS THE REALM OF JOY THAT IS RELEASED BY CHRIST JESUS, THE ALMIGHTY!!!

FOR, **HIS SACREDNESS-**
KEEPS THOSE WHO PRAY FOR A TASTE OF HIS HOLINESS AND **DIVINE GOODNESS.**

FOR, CHRIST **JESUS' GENEROSITY-**
SOOTHES THE HURTING ONES WHO **BELONG TO GOD ALMIGHTY.**

HOLY, HOLY, HOLY-
ARE THE FAITHFUL SONS AND DAUGHTERS OF GOD ALMIGHTY!!!

HOLY, HOLY, HOLY-
IS THE REALM OF JOY CALLED GOD; CHRIST JESUS, THE ALMIGHTY!!!

BARBARA SPEAKING TO GOD'S REALM OF HOLY JOY

WHISPER TO ME, O BLESSED **REALM OF SACRED JOY.** WHISPER YOUR WORDS OF HOPE, SO THAT I MAY DELIVER THEM TO **YOUR LITTLE TRUSTING GIRL AND BOY.**

FOR, **THEY TOO-**
DESIRE TO MEET AND **GREET HOLY YOU.**

HOLY, HOLY, HOLY-

The Royal Union

IS THE JOY THAT COMES WITH KNOWING AND LOVING CHRIST ALMIGHTY!!!

BARBARA SPEAKING

AS WE **MOVE CLOSER-**
TO THE NATURAL JOY THAT COMES FROM **GOD, THE ROYAL DIVINE FATHER-**

I WILL **HOLD ON TIGHT-**
TO THE HOLY GOD WHO REVEALS HIS WONDERFUL **SOOTHING LIGHT.**

WHEN THE JOY OF THE NIGHT FALLS

BARBARA SPEAKING TO EARTH'S SPIRITUALLY NEEDY RESIDENTS

WHEN THE JOY OF **THE NIGHT FALLS-**
I WILL LISTEN FOR **MY GOD HOLY CALLS.**

FOR, HE **CALLS, YOU SEE-**
THE BLESSED NAMES THAT BELONG TO **YOU AND ME.**

HOLY, HOLY, HOLY-
ARE THE CALLS OF GOD ALMIGHTY!!!

MY BLESSED SOUL **WILL RECEIVE-**

THE CALL OF ALMIGHTY GOD, SO THAT I WILL NOT **BE DECEIVED.**

FOR, SATAN'S REALM OF **DESTRUCTION-**
HAS DECEIVED SOME OF **GOD'S GREATEST CREATION.**

FOR, UNHOLY, **BUT TRUE-**
IS THE BEAST WHO TRIES TO DESTROY **ME AND YOU.**

HOLY, HOLY, HOLY-
IS THE GOD AND FATHER WHO RESCUED YOU AND ME.

MY BLESSED SPIRIT MOVES IN THE LAND OF JOY AND **DIVINE FREEDOM-**
AS ALMIGHTY GOD'S SAINTS ENTER **HIS HEAVENLY KINGDOM.**

FOR, **HOLY AND TRUE-**
IS THE GOD AND FATHER WHO RESCUED ME **AND BLESSED YOU.**

BARBARA SPEAKING TO HER BLESSED SOUL

MOVE, O BLESSED **SOUL OF MINE!**
REJOICE IN THE PRESENCE OF DIVINE ROYALTY AND GOODNESS DURING **THIS PERIOD OF TIME.**

MOVE TO **THE BEAT-**

The Royal Union

AS YOU MOVE YOUR **REJOICING FEET!**

BARBARA SPEAKING TO EARTH'S SPIRITUALLY NEEDY RESIDENTS

FOR, **HOLY AND TRUE-**
IS THE ROYAL GOD AND KING WHO SHARES THE REALM OF HEAVEN SENT JOY **WITH ALL OF YOU.**

HOLY, HOLY, HOLY-
IS THE PRAISING CHRIST ALMIGHTY!!!

I WILL EXPRESS **MY GRATITUDE-**
AS I MOVE WITH THE GREAT **HEAVENLY MULTITUDE.**

FOR, THE SOUND OF **JOYOUS PRAISE-**
TRIUMPHS IN THE PRESENCE OF ALMIGHTY GOD, DURING **THESE PRAISE WORTHY DAYS.**

MY MIND, BODY, AND SOUL CAN FEEL AND HEAR THE SILENCE

BARBARA SPEAKING

MY SOUL CAN **FEEL THE SILENCE-**
AS MY BLESSED SPIRIT BEHOLDS **GOD'S DIVINE ROYAL PRESENCE.**

I CAN HEAR THE **SILENT LAUGHTER-**

AS I SIT ON THE THRONE NEXT TO ALMIGHTY GOD, **MY REJOICING ROYAL HEAVENLY FATHER.**

I CAN SEE-
HEAVENLY THINGS THAT ARE **MADE VISIBLE TO ME.**

I CAN SEE, I CAN SEE; **I CAN REALLY SEE-**
ALL OF THE HEAVENLY THINGS THAT MANIFESTED THROUGH THE SILENCE THAT SURROUNDED **THE THRONE OF GOD ALMIGHTY.**

FOR, THE DIVINE **JOY, YOU SEE-**
WERE WITHIN MY REALM OF **SACRED VISIBILITY.**

HOLY, HOLY, HOLY-
IS THE JOY THAT SITS ON THE THRONE WITH GOD, **THE ALMIGHTY.**

FOR, HE HAS **SUMMONED, YOU SEE-**
THE ESSENCE OF SWEET JOY THAT SAT ON **THE THRONE NEXT TO ME.**

HOLY, HOLY, HOLY-
IS THE JOYFUL RESIDENT WHO SINGS SONGS OF **PRAISE TO CHRIST, THE ROYAL ALMIGHTY!!!**

FOR, MY BLESSED SPIRIT DID **WITNESS, YOU SEE-**

THE DIVINE JOY THAT OCCUPIED **THE THRONE NEXT TO ME.**

HOLY, HOLY, HOLY-
IS THE JOY THAT ACCOMPANIED GOD ALMIGHTY!!!

MOVE, O GREAT AND HOLY WINDS!

MOVE, O GREAT FORCEFUL **WINDS OF GOD ALMIGHTY!** MOVE THE SWEET ESSENCE OF DIVINE JOY THAT DESIRES TO **SIT WITH ME.**

FOR, MY HEAVENLY THRONE OF **DIVINE LOVE AND MERCY-**
SITS NEXT TO THE THRONE OF **THE ETERNAL GOD ALMIGHTY.**

FOR, **HOLY AND REAL-**
ARE THE HEAVENLY THRONES THAT **I CAN TRULY SEE AND FEEL.**

<u>**BARBARA SPEAKING TO ALMIGHTY GOD**</u>

MY HOLY GOD: YOUR REALM OF SWEET UNENDING JOY **HAS CAPTURED ME.**
IT HAS CAPTURED THE LIVING SOUL THAT WAS **SANCTIFIED BY GOD ALMIGHTY.**

FOR, I CAN **FEEL, YOU SEE-**
THE LIVING REALM OF DIVINE JOY THAT MOVES WITH **ALMIGHTY GOD AND BLESSED ME.**

HOLY, HOLY, HOLY-
IS THE JOYFUL GOD ALMIGHTY!!!

I CAN FEEL THE DIVINE JOY AS IT FLOWS THROUGHOUT **MY EARTHLY RESIDENCE.**
I CAN FEEL THE HOLY JOY AS IT REVEALS **GOD'S HOLY ROYAL PRESENCE.**

I CAN FEEL THE **HEAVENLY DELIGHT-**
AS I LOOK UP TO **MY GOD'S GLORIOUS LIGHT.**

FOR, **HOLY, YOU SEE-**
IS THE DIVINE JOY THAT HAS **CAPTIVATED BLESSED ME.**

I CAN FEEL-
THE HEAVEN SENT COMFORT THAT IS **HOLY, ETERNAL, AND REAL.**

I CAN TRULY FEEL THE HOLY PRESENCE OF ALMIGHTY GOD, **THE HOLY ETERNAL ROYAL ONE, YOU SEE-**
AS I ENJOY THE SPIRITUAL JOY AND WEALTH THAT HAVE **DESCENDED TO ME.**

The Royal Union

I ENJOY THE HEAVENLY GIFTS, YOU SEE-
THAT DESCENDED TO ME FROM MY CREATOR; GOD ALMIGHTY

HOLY, HOLY, HOLY-
IS THE REALM OF JOY THAT I RECEIVE DAILY FROM GOD, THE ALMIGHTY!!!

YOUR REALM OF DIVINE JOY HAS ENVELOPED MY BLESSED BEING-
FOR, I KNOW THAT I AM IN THE HOLY PRESENCE OF THE FOREVER-LIVING GOD AND ALMIGHTY KING.

HOLY, HOLY, HOLY-
IS THE JOY THAT COMES WITH KNOWING AND FOLLOWING CHRIST ALMIGHTY!!!

FOR, HIS JOY IS REAL-
YES! IT IS A DIVINE EXPERIENCE THAT MY MIND AND BODY CAN TRULY FEEL.

GOD'S JOY IS EVERLASTING-
FOR, IT SURROUNDS MY SPIRITUAL AND PHYSICAL BEING.

HOLY IS GOD'S DESCENDED GIFT OF JOY-
THAT BRINGS SPIRITUAL HAPPINESS TO EVERY BELIEVING GIRL AND BOY.

HOLY AND TRUE-
IS THE HEAVEN SENT JOY THAT SEES GOD'S **BLESSED ONES THROUGH.**

HOLY, HOLY, HOLY-
IS THE JOY THAT FLOWS THROUGH MY RECEPTIVE **BODY!!!**

WHEN THE REALM OF DIVINE JOY CAPTIVATES MY SOUL

<u>**BARBARA SPEAKING**</u>

WHEN THE REALM OF HEAVEN SENT JOY CAPTIVATES MY SOUL, **MY IGNITED BEING-**
RELEASES THE PRAISE AND LOVE THAT I HAVE FOR CHRIST JESUS, **MY MIGHTY GOD AND ROYAL KING.**

FOR, **HOLY, YOU SEE-**
IS THE JOY OF KNOWING GOD, THE FATHER'S, ONLY BEGOTTEN SON; **CHRIST JESUS, THE ALMIGHTY.**

FOR, **HOLY AND TRUE-**
IS THE GOD WHO **LOVES ME AND YOU.**

HOLY, HOLY, HOLY-
IS THE REALM OF JOY CALLED GOD ALMIGHTY!!!

The Royal Union

THE HEAVEN SENT JOY PERMEATES MY BODY AND SOUL

BARBARA SPEAKING

GOD'S HEAVEN SENT JOY FLOWS THROUGH MY BODY AND SOUL IN THE MIDST OF **LIFE'S HAPPENINGS-** HIS JOY FLOWS THROUGH MY BEING WHEN I'M IN THE HOLY PRESENCE OF CHRIST **JESUS, THE ROYAL KING OF KINGS.**

GOD'S REALM OF JOY COMFORTS MY SOUL WHENEVER THE REALM OF **EVIL AND DESTRUCTION-** TORTURES GOD'S **EARTHLY CHILDREN.**

FOR, **HOLY, YOU SEE-**
IS THE HEAVEN DESCENDED JOY THAT TRAVELS WITH **BLESSED ME.**

DIVINE SPIRITUAL JOY

JOY, JOY, SPIRITUAL JOY- IS RELEASED FROM THE **THRONE OF GOD ALMIGHTY.**
IT IS RELEASED BY THE GOD AND FATHER OF **DIVINE ROYALTY.**

SPIRITUAL JOY-
IS THE GRACE THAT IS OFFERED TO THE FAITHFUL **LITTLE GIRL AND BOY.**

FOR, **HOLY, YOU SEE-**
IS THE GOD AND FATHER WHO **CREATED YOU AND ME.**

I WILL FULLY **RECEIVE, YOU SEE-**
THE JOYFUL BLESSINGS THAT ARE SENT FROM SWEET HEAVEN TO **GOD'S EARTHLY CHILDREN AND ME.**

FOR, **HOLY AND TRUE-**
IS THE JOY THAT GOD, THE FATHER, **SENDS TO ME AND YOU.**

LET GOD'S HOLY BELLS RING!!!

BARBARA SPEAKING

LET THE HOLY BELLS OF SWEET HEAVEN **RELEASE ITS SILENT RING!**
FOR, HEAVEN AND EARTH ARE IN THE PRESENCE OF CHRIST **JESUS, THE DIVINE ROYAL ETERNAL GOD AND KING.**

LET GOD'S **HOLY BELL RING-**
FOR, THE REALM OF DIVINE JOY HAS ENTERED THE HOME OF BARBARA, THE HEAVEN SENT DEVOTED MESSENGER OF CHRIST JESUS, **HEAVEN'S AND EARTH'S FORETOLD GLORIOUS TRIUMPHANT KING.**

The Royal Union

RING, O BLESSED BELL!
RELEASE THE UNTOLD STORY THAT **YOU MUST TELL!**

RELEASE YOUR **HEAVENLY SOUND-**
SO THAT CHRIST JESUS' EARTHLY AND HEAVENLY SUBJECTS WILL KNOW THAT **HIS HOLY SPIRIT AND PRESENCE ARE ALWAYS AROUND.**

RING, O BLESSED **BELLS, RING!**
JOIN GOD'S HOLY HEAVENLY CHOIRS AS THEY LIFT UP THEIR **JOYFUL VOICES AND SING.**

RING **LOUD AND CLEAR-**
SO THAT YOU MAY CONQUER EARTH'S **LINGERING REALM OF FEAR.**

RING IN THE PRESENCE OF **DIVINE GOODNESS-**
AS YOU RECEIVE A **TASTE OF GOD'S HOLINESS!**

RING, RING, RING!
LET CHRIST, THE LORD, DO **HIS HOLY THING!**

FOR, THE WITNESSES HAVE **ARRIVED, YOU SEE-**
SO THAT THEY MAY EXPERIENCE THE JOY AND BLISS THAT COME WITH BEHOLDING **THE PRESENCE OF DIVINE ROYALTY.**

LET THE HOLY **BELLS RING-**

LET THE JOY FILLED **CHOIRS SING!**

FOR, THE ANNOUNCEMENT HAS BEEN **MADE, YOU SEE-**
AND NOW, WE ARE ALL IN THE PRESENCE OF **DIVINE ROYALTY!**

BOW, O INVITED GUESTS, BOW-
FOR YOU WILL EXPERIENCE DIVINE **GLORY RIGHT NOW!!!**

BOW, **O INVITED ONE!**
FOR YOU ARE IN THE HOLY PRESENCE OF GOD, THE FATHER'S, **ONLY BEGOTTEN ROYAL SON.**

BOW, ALL YOU **BLESSED ONES-**
FOR YOU ARE ALMIGHTY GOD'S **INVITED DAUGHTERS AND SONS!**

YOU WILL NOW EXPERIENCE FROM **THE ROYAL KING OF KINGS-**
HEAVEN'S GREAT **KNOWLEDGE AND TIDINGS.**

REJOICE, O BLESSED **GATES OF SWEET HEAVEN!**
FOR, YOU ARE IN THE PRESENCE OF **ALMIGHTY GOD AND HIS BLESSED CHOSEN.**

THERE ARE MANY JOY FILLED DAYS

The Royal Union

THERE **ARE MANY-**
JOYFUL DAYS FOR THE BLESSED ONES OF **GOD ALMIGHTY.**

THERE ARE MANY **JOY FILLED DAYS-**
THAT EXIST IN THE MIDST OF THE BLESSED ONES **CONTINUOUS PRAISE.**

FOR, **THE HALLELUJAHS-**
SURROUND THE MIGHTY THRONE **THAT IS JEHOVAH'S.**

FOR, THE DIVINE JOY THAT HEAVEN'S RESIDENTS **EXPRESS, YOU SEE-**
IS APPROVED BY THE ONE AND ONLY **GOD ALMIGHTY.**

FOR, HIS SACRED REALM OF **UNENDING JOY-**
SHINES ON THE BEINGS OF GOD'S BLESSED **BELIEVING GIRL AND BOY.**

HOLY, HOLY, HOLY-
IS THE JOY THAT SURROUNDS THE THRONE OF THE ROYAL CHRIST ALMIGHTY

FOR, THE **JOYFUL PRAISE-**
ENCOMPASSES HEAVEN'S **UNENDING DAYS.**

HOLY, HOLY, HOLY-
IS THE PRAISE WORTHY KING; CHRIST ALMIGHTY!!!

FOR, HIS HEAVEN **SENT BLESSINGS-**
ARE GIFTS THAT HAVE LEFT THE MIGHTY THRONE
OF CHRIST JESUS, **THE ROYAL AND ETERNAL KING
OF KINGS.**

HOLY, HOLY, HOLY-
IS THE FOREVER REIGNING KING ALMIGHTY!!!

              AND WE WILL BOW

AND WE WILL CONSTANTLY **BOW, YOU SEE-**
IN THE HOLY PRESENCE OF ALMIGHTY GOD WHO IS
THE **UNENDING REALM OF SWEET DIVINITY.**

HOLY, ETERNAL **AND TRUE-**
ARE THE ROYAL ONES WHO HAVE OFFERED TO
SERVE ALL OF YOU.

HOLY, HOLY, HOLY-
**ARE THE CHOSEN BLESSED CHILDREN OF THE ROYAL
GOD ALMIGHTY!!!**

**DIVINE JOY HAS ENTERED THE DINING ROOM OF THE
ROYAL FAMILY**

DIVINE JOY HAS ENTERED THE DINING ROOM OF **THE
ROYAL FAMILY-**

The Royal Union

IT HAS SURROUNDED THE ONLY BEGOTTEN SON AND THE INVITED GUESTS OF GOD, THE **ROYAL DIVINE FATHER, ALMIGHTY.**

IT HAS PERMEATED THE ENTIRE DINING **ROOM, YOU SEE-**
FOR, IT TOO, WAS INVITED BY THE GRACIOUS **ROYAL GOD ALMIGHTY.**

HOLY, YOU SEE-
IS THE JOY THAT WAS RELEASED IN THE PRESENCE OF ALMIGHTY **GOD'S INVITED COMPANY.**

FOR, THE GOD **ORCHESTRATED JOY-**
FLOWS THROUGH THE DANCE HALL WHERE THE REALM OF **EVIL CANNOT ENTER NOR DESTROY.**

HOLY, HOLY, HOLY-
IS THE FLOWING REALMS OF INAUDIBLE JOY THAT WAS RELEASED AND ORDERED BY THE LIVING **ROYAL ALMIGHTY!!!**

HOLY, HOLY, HOLY-
IS THE INAUDIBLE SOUNDS THAT COME FROM THE HOSTS OF DIVINE **ROYALTY!!**

BOOK # SIX

IF ONLY YOU KNEW

IF ONLY YOU KNEW

BY:

BARBARA ANN MARY MACK

BEGAN: OCTOBER 29, 2024

COMPLETED: NOVEMBER 6, 2024

INTRODUCTION

I AM ALMIGHTY GOD:
I AM THE ONE AND ONLY ALL KNOWING ROYAL ONE;
AND THE ORIGIN OF DIVINE PURE LOVE.

I AM SWEET ETERNITY-
FOR THERE IS NO ONE BEFORE ME.

I AM HE WHO CALLED EXISTENCE INTO SWEET EXISTENCE

I AM EXISTENCE-
BEHOLD, O INVITED GUESTS; BEHOLD MY ETERNAL ROYAL PRESENCE.

I AM HE WHO MOVES IN SWEET HEAVEN; AND I AM HE WHO MOVES IN THE MIDST OF EARTH'S INHABITANTS TODAY.
BEHOLD: I AM THE ONLY LIFE SAVING WAY.

I AM THE LIGHT, WHICH SHINES THROUGHOUT THE DAY.
I AM HE WHO LEADS THE VALUABLE ONES TO MY LIFE REWARDING HOLY WAY.

I DO EXIST: I DO EXIST; I AM THE ALL KNOWING GOD WHO DOES EXIST.

BEHOLD ME, DEAR CHILDREN; FOR I AM IN YOUR MIDST.

BEHOLD THE ORIGIN OF LIFE.

BEHOLD HE WHO RULES OVER THE BELIEVING HUSBAND AND HIS VALUABLE CHILDREN AND WIFE.

HOLY, YOU SEE-
IS MY REALM OF DIVINE ROYALTY.

BEHOLD THE ONE AND ONLY-
CHRIST JESUS, THE ETERNAL GOD ALMIGHTY.

BEHOLD THE OMNIPRESENT ONE-
BEHOLD CHRIST JESUS, FOR, I AM TRULY GOD, THE FATHER'S, ONLY BEGOTTEN SON.

BEHOLD ME-
LOOK UPON THE HOLY ESSENCE OF HEAVENLY ROYALTY.

DEAR CHILDREN: IF ONLY YOU KNEW ME, THE FOREVER-LIVING CHRIST JESUS, THE ALMIGHTY

DEAR CHILDREN:
I AM SPEAKING TO THOSE FROM EVERY NATION.

IF ONLY-
YOU KNEW **ETERNAL ROYAL ME.**

IF ONLY-
YOU WOULD FOLLOW IN THE FOOTSTEPS OF THE FOREVER-**LIVING CHRIST ALMIGHTY.**

IF ONLY-
YOU COULD SEE VALUABLE AND **EVERLASTING GOD ALMIGHTY.**

IF ONLY, IF ONLY, IF ONLY-
YOU WOULD RECEIVE **MY BLESSED SPIRIT THAT IS EVERLASTING AND HOLY**

I WOULD **GIVE TO YOU-**
A LOVE THAT IS **ETERNAL AND TRUE.**

LET US-
WALK IN THE LIGHT OF THE FOREVER **REIGNING CHRIST JESUS.**

FOR, WITHIN **HIS HOLY LIGHT-**
YOU WILL RECEIVE **A GLORIOUS SIGHT.**

FOR, **HOLY AND TRUE-**
IS THE MAGNIFICENT LIGHT THAT **SHINES UPON BLESSED YOU.**

HOLY, HOLY, HOLY-
IS THE LIVING LIGHT CALLED GOD ALMIGHTY!!!

DEAR CHILDREN: COME CLOSER-
SO THAT YOU MAY GET A TASTE OF ALMIGHTY GOD, YOUR HEAVENLY **SAVIOR AND ROYAL FATHER.**

FOR, **HOLY, YOU SEE-**
IS YOUR HEAVEN DESCENDED GOD AND SAVIOR; **CHRIST ALMIGHTY.**

IF ONLY YOU KNEW-
HOW MUCH YOUR CREATOR AND **GOD LOVES YOU.**

HOLY, HOLY, HOLY-
IS THE LOVE THAT COMES FROM GOD ALMIGHTY!!!

YOU, O HOLY GOD, KNOW EVERYTHING

BARBARA SPEAKING TO THE ROYAL GOD ALIGHTY

YOU, O HOLY GOD, **KNOW EVERYTHING-**
FOR, YOU ARE THE NEW BIRTH CALLED **CHRIST, THE ROYAL KING.**

AS I SAY-
THE HOLY WORDS THAT SPEAK OF YOUR **LIFE REWARDING WAY-**

I WILL **REMEMBER-**
THAT YOU ARE THE ROYAL ALL-KNOWING **GOD, THE FATHER.**

I WILL LISTEN **AND HEAR-**
YOUR HOLY WORDS THAT **ARE VERY NEAR.**

ALMIGHTY GOD SPEAKING TO BARBARA

DEAR BARBARA: **IF ONLY YOU KNEW-**
THE DEPTH OF THE LOVE THAT I HAVE FOR MY EARTHLY LOVED ONES **AND BLESSED YOU.**

DEAR BARBARA:
IF ONLY YOU KNEW OF THE GREAT LOVE THAT COMES FROM **ALMIGHTY GOD, YOUR HEAVENLY FATHER.**

YOU WOULD **UNDERSTAND**-
THE HOLY WORKS THAT COME FROM MY POWERFUL **LIFE-SAVING HAND.**

DEAR DAUGHTER: IF ONLY YOU COULD **SEE AND FEEL**-
A POWERFUL LOVE THAT IS **HOLY AND REAL.**

THEN YOU **WOULD KNOW**-
OF THE LOVE THAT SECURES YOU **WHEREVER YOU GO.**

LISTEN. LISTEN. LISTEN.
LISTEN TO MY HOLY VOICE AS YOU SPEAK FOR ME **TO MY VULNERABLE CHILDREN.**

DEAR BARBARA: **TELL THEM FOR ME**-
THAT THE LOVE THAT I OFFER IS **EVERLASTING AND FREE.**

TELL THEM **FOR ME**-
THAT MY LOVE HAS TRAVELED FROM THE ESSENCE THAT CALLED INTO EXISTENCE **THE REALM OF SWEET ETERNITY.**

Barbara Ann Mary Mack

DEAR BARBARA: TELL MY NEEDY CHILDREN **FOR ME-**
THAT I AM THE REALM **CALLED INFINITY.**

TELL THEM, **DEAR BARBARA-**
FOR, I, ALONE, HOLD THE KEY THAT WILL OPEN THE GATES THAT LEAD TO **THE REALM OF SWEET TOMORROW.**

FOR, IF ONLY **THEY KNEW-**
HOW MUCH I LOVE MY **EARTHLY OFFSPRING AND YOU.**

THEY WOULD **BE AWARE-**
OF THE GOD WHO **DOES CARE.**

FOR, **HOLY AND TRUE-**
IS THE GOD AND LORD WHO **SENT BLESSED YOU.**

MY LOVE IS ETERNAL AND TRUE, SAYS THE LORD GOD

ALMIGHTY GOD SPEAKING

DEAR **CHILDREN:**
YES, YOU FROM EVERY **BLESSED NATION.**

BELIEVE THIS **FROM ME-**
BELIEVE THAT MY LOVE IS **EVERLASTING AND FREE.**

The Royal Union

MY LOVE IS ETERNAL, **AND IT IS TRUE**-
IT IS A DIVINE LOVE THAT **WILL RESCUE.**

FOR, MY **SINKING ONES**-
ARE MY SOUGHT FOR **DAUGHTERS AND SONS.**

FOR, **MY LOVE**-
DESCENDED FROM MY **MIGHTY THRONE ABOVE.**

ONLY THE REALM OF SWEET HEAVENLY **KNOWLEDGE, YOU SEE**-
COULD RELEASE THE LOVE THAT COMES FROM **THE ROYAL ALMIGHTY.**

FOR, ETERNAL **AND TRUE**-
IS THE GOD WHO TRULY LOVES **HIS CREATION AND YOU.**

HOLY, HOLY, HOLY-
IS THE LOVE THAT COMES WITH KNOWING CHRIST JESUS, **THE ALMIGHTY!!!**

FOR, IF **YOU ONLY**-
KNEW OF THE DEPTH OF THE LOVE THAT DESCENDED WITH **CHRIST JESUS, THE ALMIGHTY.**

HOLY, HOLY, HOLY-

IS THE LOVE THAT WAS RELEASED FROM THE HOME OF GOD ALMIGHTY!!!

FOR, THE REALM OF DIVINE **LOVE, YOU SEE**-
DESCENDED FROM SWEET **HEAVEN WITH ME.**

DEAR CHILDREN-
O BLESSED ONES FROM **EVERY BLESSED NATION.**

IF ONLY YOU KNEW-
OF THE LOVE THAT **I HAVE FOR YOU.**

YOU WOULD GLADLY **REPENT, YOU SEE**-
IN THE HOLY PRESENCE OF **GOD ALMIGHTY.**

IF YOU ONLY KNEW-
HOW MUCH YOUR **HOLY GOD LOVES YOU.**

YOU WOULD **NEVER DENY**-
THE LOVE THAT COMES FROM **ABOVE THE BRIGHT BLUE SKY.**

FOR, **HOLY, YOU SEE**-
IS THE LOVE THAT COMES FROM **BLESSED LIFE GIVING ME.**

IF ONLY YOU KNEW-

OF THE DEPTH OF THE LOVE THAT **I TRULY HAVE FOR YOU.**

FOR, **HOLY AND REAL-**
IS THE SACRED LOVE THAT **NO ONE COULD STEAL.**

IF ONLY THEY KNEW

BARBARA SPEAKING TO ALMIGHTY GOD, THE DIVINE ROYAL ONE

MY GOD: **IF THEY ONLY KNEW-**
HOW MUCH THAT **I TRULY LOVE HOLY YOU.**

IF THEY ONLY KNEW-
ALL OF THE GLORIOUS THINGS **THAT YOU DO.**

IF ONLY THEY **COULD SEE-**
ALL OF THE WONDERFUL THINGS THAT ARE CALLED INTO EXISTENCE BY **GOD, THE ALMIGHTY.**

IF THEY **COULD KNOW-**
THAT YOU ARE WITH ME WHEREVER MY BLESSED **SOUL AND BODY GO.**

IF THEY COULD **ONLY FEEL-**
THE DIVINE LOVE THAT IS **ETERNAL AND REAL.**

IF ONLY. IF ONLY-

IF ONLY THEY KNEW THAT YOU AND I HAVE A LOVE THAT IS **EVERLASTING AND TRUE.**

I WANT **EVERYONE-**
TO KNOW ABOUT THE LOVELY UNION THAT I SHARE WITH **GOD, THE FATHER'S, ONLY BEGOTTEN SON.**

I WANT THE WHOLE WIDE **WORLD TO SEE-**
THAT THE LOVE THAT WE SHARE IS A PART OF **THIS WORLD'S UNENDING HISTORY.**

I WANT THE **WORLD TO SHARE-**
THE KNOWLEDGE THAT YOU REVEAL TO THOSE **WHO REALLY CARE.**

FOR, **IF THEY ONLY KNEW-**
OF THE LOVE THAT DESCENDED TO THE **CALLED AND CHOSEN FEW.**

IF ONLY **THEY COULD SEE-**
THE HOLY WORKS OF ALMIGHTY GOD, THE BLESSED **AND BELOVED TRINITY.**

IF THEY WOULD **ONLY LISTEN-**
TO THE HOLY MESSAGES THAT GOD HAS FOR **HIS BLESSED EARTHLY CHILDREN.**

IF ONLY. IF ONLY. IF ONLY-

The Royal Union

THEY COULD BEHOLD THE HOLY PRESENCE OF **GOD, THE ALMIGHTY!!!**

MY HOLY GOD: **IF ONLY THEY KNEW-**
OF THE DIVINE LOVE THAT **IS ETERNAL AND TRUE.**

THEN, THEY **WOULD SEE-**
THE DIVINE LOVE THAT EXISTS BETWEEN **YOU AND ME.**

IF ONLY. IF ONLY. IF ONLY-
IF ONLY THEY COULD SEE AND FEEL THE DIVINE UNION THAT I HAVE WITH CHRIST JESUS, THE ETERNAL KING, GOD, AND **ONLY BEGOTTEN SON OF GOD, THE FATHER, ALMIGHTY.**

FOR, **HOLY, YOU SEE-**
IS THE HEAVENLY LOVE THAT HAS **UNITED WITH BLESSED ME.**

MY GLORIOUS GOD: IF ONLY YOUR EARTHLY **LOVED ONES KNEW-**
HOW MUCH THEY RECEIVE DAILY FROM THE GOD WHO **IS ETERNAL AND TRUE.**

IF WE ONLY KNEW-
OF THE DEPTH OF GENUINE LOVE THAT **COMES FROM EVERLASTING YOU.**

IF ONLY WE COULD **UNDERSTAND-**
THE DIVINE POWER THAT EMITS FROM YOUR **HOLY UNCHANGING ROYAL HAND.**

FOR, YOUR LOVE **MAGNIFIES, YOU SEE-**
THE REALM OF DIVINE HOPE THAT YOU GIVE TO THE CHILDREN WHO **BELONG TO GOD, THE ALMIGHTY.**

FOR, YOUR LOVE IS **GREAT AND UNENDING-**
IT IS A DIVINE LOVE THAT IS RELEASED FROM THE HEAVENLY THRONE THAT HOLDS THE ROYAL BEING OF CHRIST JESUS, OUR HEAVENLY AND **EARTHLY GOD AND KING.**

IF ONLY WE **COULD BEHOLD-**
A LOVE THAT SHINES BRIGHTER THAN FRESHLY FORMED **SILVER AND GOLD.**

FOR, YOUR **FINE SILVER-**
IS CALLED INTO EXISTENCE BY THE ONE AND ONLY **GOD AND SAVIOR.**

HOLY, HOLY, HOLY-
ARE THE SILVER AND GOLD THAT ARE FORMED BY GOD, THE ROYAL ALMIGHTY!!!

The Royal Union

BOOK # SEVEN

GOD'S HOLY STARS AND ME

GOD'S HOLY STARS AND ME

BY:

BARBARA ANN MARY MACK

BEGAN: OCTOBER 30, 2024

COMPLETED: NOVEMBER 6, 2024

INTRODUCTION

THE HEAVENLY HOLY STARS, YOU SEE-
WERE CALLED INTO EXISTENCE BY THE ONE AND ONLY GOD ALMIGHTY.

OH, HOW CREATIVE IS HE-
TO CALL INTO EXISTENCE THE BEAUTY THAT IS AT A DISTENCE FROM YOU AND ME.

FOR, THE HEAVENLY FORMED STAR-
IN REALITY, ISN'T VERY FAR.

FOR, MY EYES CAN TRULY SEE-
THE UNIVERSE AND ITS DIVINE BEAUTY.

HOLY, HOLY, HOLY-
ARE THE HEAVENLY BEAUTIFUL STARS THAT WERE CALLED INTO EXISTENCE BY THE ONE AND ONLY GOD ALMIGHTY!!!

THE DIVINE BEAUTY THAT SURROUNDS GOD'S UNIVERSE; AND THE BRILLIANCE OF THE STARS

THERE ARE **MANY, YOU SEE-**
OF STARS THAT WERE CALLED INTO EXISTENCE BY **GOD, THE ALMIGHTY.**

FOR, THE **NUMBER ONE-**
REVEALS THE HEAVENLY WORKS OF GOD, THE FATHER'S, **ONLY BEGOTTEN SON.**

FOR, THERE **ARE MANY-**
THAT WERE FORMED BY THE HOLY HANDS OF **SWEET ETERNITY.**

FOR, THE HEAVENLY **KING, YOU SEE-**
NUMBERED THE STARS THAT **DANCED BEFORE ME.**

HOLY, HOLY, HOLY-
ARE THE STARS THAT WERE PLACED BEFORE ME.

FOR, THEIR **FORMATION-**
SALUTED EVERY **WORTHY NATION.**

FOR, **HOLY AND REAL-**
ARE THE STARS AND UNIVERSE THAT I CAN **TRULY SEE AND FEEL.**
HOLY, HOLY, HOLY-
ARE THE DANCING STARS THAT WERE CALLED INTO EXISTENCE BY GOD ALMIGHTY!!!

I CAN **ALSO SEE-**
THE WANDERING CHILDREN OF GOD ALMIGHTY, FOR, THEY WANTED TO BE FREE LIKE **THE HEAVENLY STARS AND ME.**

HOLY, HOLY, HOLY-
ARE THE GREAT CREATIONS OF GOD ALMIGHTY!!!

THE STAR, THE STAR; THE SWEETEST **HEAVEN LIT STAR.**
ALTHOUGH IT TRAVELS WITH GREAT SPEED, ITS EXISTENCE **ISN'T VERY FAR.**

OH HOW GREAT OF **A DELIGHT-**
TO WITNESS AN UNEARTHLY CREATION THAT EXHIBITS GOD'S **INTERVENTION AND HOLY MIGHT.**

FOR, **ITS EXISTENCE-**
CONFIRMS GOD **HOLY ROYAL PRESENCE.**

BARBARA SPEAKING TO THE HEAVENLY STAR

MOVE, O BLESSED **HEAVEN MADE ONE.**
MOVE WITH GREAT SPEED IN THE PRESENCE OF **GOD, THE FATHER'S, ONLY BEGOTTEN SON.**

TRAVEL **WITH ME-**
THROUGH **GOD'S BLESSED GALAXY.**

FOR, THE REALM OF **UNENDING TIME, YOU SEE-**
HAS CAPTIVATED THE HOUSEHOLD OF **DIVINE ROYALTY.**

MOVE WITH MY BLESSED IGNITED BEING, **O HEAVEN FORMED STAR.**
MOVE WITH ME WITHIN THE REALM THAT DOESN'T **TRAVEL TOO FAR.**

FOR, **HOLY, YOU SEE-**
IS THE HEAVENLY HOUSEHOLD OF **DIVINE ROYALTY.**

MOVE, MOVE, MOVE WITHIN **HEAVEN'S IGNITED GALAXY.**
MOVE WITH ME, O BLESSED STAR, AS YOU BEHOLD **THE PRESENCE OF DIVINE ROYALTY.**

FOR, **HOLY AND TRUE-**
IS THE GOD WHO **CREATED ME AND YOU.**

MY BLESSED SPIRIT HAS TRAVELED THROUGH GOD'S UNKNOWN TERRITORY

BARBARA SPEAKING

MY BLESSED EXCITED SPIRIT HAS TRAVELED THROUGH **GOD'S UNKNOWN AND UNFAMILIAR TERRITORY.**
YES! MY BLESSED SPIRIT HAS SOARED THROUGH **THE FULLY UNKNOWN GALAXY.**

FOR, MY SPIRIT **DESIRED TO SEE-**
ALL OF THE UNKNOWN THINGS THAT WERE CREATED AND CALLED INTO EXISTENCE **BY THE ALL-POWERFUL GOD ALMIGHTY.**

FOR, **HOLY, YOU SEE-**
IS THE CREATOR OF **THE HEAVEN'S GALAXY**

HOLY IS THE **UNKNOWN WORLD-**
THAT BRINGS ABOUT AN INTERESTED AND CURIOUS **BOY AND GIRL.**

FOR, MANKIND'S LIMITED **KNOWLEDGE, YOU SEE-**
DOESN'T REALLY CLARIFY, NOR EXPLAIN THE ENTIRE EXISTENCE OF **THE VISIBLE GALAXY.**

FOR, THE HEAVENLY **BODIES, YOU SEE-**

WERE CALLED INTO EXISTENCE BY THE **ALL-POWERFUL GOD ALMIGHTY.**

CLOSER TO THE REALM OF DIVINE PURITY

BARBARA SPEAKING

MY BLESSED SPIRIT MOVES CLOSER TO THE REALM OF DIVINE PURITY-
CLOSER TO THE GOD WHO FORMED HIS BLESSED EARTHLY LOVED ONES AND ME.

I WILL MOVE CLOSER, YOU SEE-
SO THAT MY BLESSED SOUL MAY GET A GLIMPSE OF MY SAVIOR AND GOD ALMIGHTY.

I WILL MOVE IN THE DIRECTION OF HIS REALM OF HEAVENLY HOLINESS-
SO THAT MY BLESSED SPIRIT MAY INHALE HIS DIVINE GOODNESS.

FOR, HOLY, YOU SEE-
IS THE GOD AND CREATOR OF THE HEAVEN'S SWEET GALAXY.

BARBARA SPEAKING TO ALMIGHTY GOD

I WILL MOVE IN THE PRESENCE OF **YOUR BRIGHTEST STAR-**
SO THAT I MAY EXPERIENCE THE DIVINE WARMTH OF **THE GOD AND CREATOR WHO ISN'T VERY FAR.**

FOR, **HOLY, YOU SEE-**
ARE GOD'S MAGNIFICENT **BRIGHTEST STAR AND ME.**

AS I OBSERVE THE MOON'S MAGNIFICENCE

BARBARA SPEAKING

AS MY BLESSED SOUL OBSERVES THE **MOON'S MAGNIFICENCE-**
I CAN FEEL ITS CREATOR'S **HOLY ROYAL PRESENCE.**

WHEN MY SOUL AND SPIRIT OBSERVE THE MOON DURING **THE MIDNIGHT HOUR-**
I CAN REALLY FEEL **GOD'S HOLY POWER.**

FOR, **HOLY, YOU SEE-**
IS THE GOD AND CREATOR OF **THE HEAVENLY GALAXY.**

WHEN I OBSERVE **THE MOON'S BRILLIANCE-**
I BECOME CAPTIVATED BY **ITS HEAVENLY PRESENCE.**

GOD'S GREAT PLANET EARTH HAS GIVEN ITS SECOND BIRTH

BARBARA SPEAKING

GOD'S GREAT **PLANET EARTH-**
HAS GIVEN **ITS SECOND BIRTH.**

FOR, CHRIST **JESUS, THE ALMIGHTY-**
DWELLS WITHIN **EARTHLY ME.**

THE PLANET **EARTH, YOU SEE-**
HOLDS THE LOVED ONES WHO WERE CALLED AND CHOSEN BY **GOD, THE ALMIGHTY.**

FOR, **HOLY AND TRUE-**
IS THE GOD WHO CALLED THE PLANET EARTH INTO EXISTENCE **AND BLESSED YOU.**

HOLY, HOLY, HOLY-
IS THE GREAT CREATOR CALLED GOD ALMIGHTY!!!

FOR, HE HAS **CREATED, YOU SEE-**
EVERYTHING THAT IS **GOOD AND DIVINELY.**

HOLY, HOLY, HOLY-
ARE THE MAGNIFICENT CREATIONS OF GOD ALMIGHTY!!!

The Royal Union

BOOK # EIGHT

REALITY: SWEET, SWEET, REALITY

REALITY: SWEET, SWEET, REALITY

BY:

BARBARA ANN MARY MACK

BEGAN: OCTOBER 29, 2024

COMPLETD: NOVEMBER 7, 2024

A TASTE OF SWEET HEAVENLY REALITY

BARBARA SPEAKING

REALITY; SWEET REALITY-
HAS CALLED INTO EXISTENCE THE MESSENGER AND **DAUGHTER (BARBARA) OF GOD ALMIGHTY.**

FOR, OUR EXISTENCE, **YOU SEE-**
HAS BROUGHT INTO EXISTENCE ALMIGHTY GOD'S **HOLY UNITED ROYAL STORY.**

FOR, **I, BARBARA-**
HAVE BEEN CHOSEN TO DELIVER THE GOOD NEWS THAT IS REVEALED BY **ALMIGHTY GOD, THE FATHER.**

FOR, **HOLY, YOU SEE-**
IS THE GOOD NEWS THAT **HE SHARES WITH ME.**

HOLY, HOLY, HOLY-
IS THE UNENDING REALM CALLED SWEET REALITY!!!

HOLY, HOLY, HOLY-
IS THE REALITY OF GOD ALMIGHTY!!!

FOR, HE **LIVES, YOU SEE-**

IN THE PURIFIED BEING THAT **BELONGS TO ME.**

DEAR BLESSED **FRIENDS OF MINE-**
HE IS THE REALITY THAT WILL COVER US UNTIL THE END OF **OUR BLESSED TIME.**

FOR, **HE IS REAL-**
HIS EXISTENCE, **WE CAN SURELY FEEL.**

STEP INTO **HIS WORLD-**
SO THAT HIS HOLY EXISTENCE MAY GUIDE EVERY **EARTHLY BOY AND GIRL.**

STEP INTO HIS REALM **OF SWEET REALITY-**
FOR, YOU ARE A LIVING WITNESS TO THE EXISTENCE OF **CHRIST JESUS, THE ALMIGHTY.**

LOOK UP, AND **YOU WILL SEE-**
THE REALM THAT **EXPRESSES DIVINE REALITY.**

LOOK **AROUND YOU-**
AND YOU WILL FEEL THE HOLY PRESENCE OF THE ONLY GOD WHO IS **HOLY, ETERNAL, AND TRUE.**

YOU WILL **SEE AND FIND-**
A GENUINE LOVE THAT IS **ONE OF A KIND.**

HE IS REAL, **DEAR BROTHER-**

HE IS ALIVE, **DEAR SISTER!**

HE IS IN THE MIDST OF THE LOVED ONES OF GOD, THE MAGNIFICENT, **AND ALL-POWERFUL FATHER.**
REACH FOR HIS HOLY PRESENCE; FOR **THERE IS NO OTHER!!!**

DEAR ONES: YOU ARE **NEVER ALONE-**
FOR, HIS HOLY PRESENCE MOVES IN THE MIDST OF **THE WEAK AND THE STRONG.**

WALK WITH HIM, TALK TO HIM: MOVE, MOVE, MOVE IN THE HOLY PRESENCE OF ALMIGHTY GOD, **THE EXISTING ONE.**
MOVE IN THE ROYAL PRESENCE OF CHRIST JESUS. FOR HE IS **GOD, THE ETERNAL LIVING SON.**

MOVE IN **HIS HOLY MIDST-**
FOR, HIS HOLY PRESENCE AND **POWER TRULY EXIST.**

HE IS THE REALM OF SWEET **UNENDING REALITY.**
HE IS THE LIVING GOD WHO SETS OUR **CAPTIVE SOULS FREE.**

HE IS OF **THE ROYAL LIVING-**
FOR, HE IS CHRIST JESUS, OUR **EVERLASTING GOD AND KING.**

The Royal Union

HE IS THE HOLY **ROYAL RULER-**
OVER HIS BELOVED **SON AND DAUGHTER.**

HE IS **THE SALVATION-**
THAT IS OFFERED TO HIS LOVED ONES **FROM EVERY NATION.**

HE IS THE LIVING **FINE GOLD-**
HE IS THE UNENDING STORY THAT **WILL BE TOLD.**

HE MOVES THROUGHOUT **THE EARTH-**
IN THE PRESENCE OF NEW LIFE AND **HIS SACRED BIRTH.**

HE MOVES WITH **THE TEACHING ONES-**
HE MOVES WITH HIS FAITHFUL **DAUGHTERS AND SONS.**

FOR, HE IS THE HOLY **REWARDING ONE-**
WHO GIVES EVERLASTING LIFE TO HIS **WEARY DAUGHTER AND SON.**

HE IS **REAL-**
HE IS THE LIFE THAT **NO ONE CAN STEAL.**

HOLY IS HE-
ETERNAL IS HIS POSITION **OF ROYALTY.**

Barbara Ann Mary Mack

DEAR FRIENDS: WALK WITH THE FOREVER-**LIVING CHRIST JESUS.**
WALK WITH THE LIVING REALITY WHO **SAVES THE LIVING RIGHTEOUS.**

FOR, HE RULES AND REIGNS IN **OUR BLESSED MIDST-** AS HE CONQUERS SATAN'S REALM OF EVIL WITH **HIS DIVINE FIST.**

HOLY, HOLY, HOLY-
IS THE IRON FIST OF CHRIST JESUS, THE ALMIGHTY!!!

FOR, HIS SACRED REALM OF **EXISTENCE-**
REVEALS HIS **UNENDING PERSISTENCE.**

FOR HE **PERSISTS, YOU SEE-**
IN THE ROYAL PRESENCE OF **GOD, THE FATHER, ALMIGHTY!!!**

HOLY, HOLY, HOLY-
IS THE CARE THAT WE RECEIVE FROM GOD, THE ALMIGHTY!!!

HE PERSISTS, **YOU SEE-**
IN THE CARE OF **EARTH'S VULNERABLE NEEDY.**

HE NEVER **GIVES UP ON US-**

The Royal Union

FOR WE ARE TRULY THE OFFSPRING OF THE FOREVER LIVING **CHRIST JESUS.**

HOLY, HOLY, HOLY-
IS ALMIGHTY GOD, OUR REALM OF SWEET REALITY!!!

HOLY IS **HIS ROYAL FACE-**
EVERLASTING IS **HIS HUMAN RACE.**

FOR, HE IS **THE OVERSEER-**
OF THE RACE OF PEOPLE WHO ARE FAITHFUL AND OBEDIENT TO **ALMIGHTY GOD, THE FATHER.**

HOLY, HOLY, HOLY-
IS THE SANCTIFIED RACE THAT BELONGS TO CHRIST JESUS, THE ALMIGHTY!!!

FOR, HE **GOVERNS, YOU SEE-**
THE HEAVENLY AND EARTHLY **CHILDREN OF GOD ALMIGHTY.**

HOLY, **YOU SEE-**
IS CHRIST JESUS, THE REALM OF **SWEET REALITY.**

FOR, HE **DOES EXIST-**
IN OUR **BLESSED MIDST.**

    AND, I WAS CALLED TO SERVE THE NEEDY

BARBARA SPEAKING

I WAS CALLED TO **SERVE THE NEEDY**-
THOSE WHO ARE FAITHFUL TO **GOD ALMIGHTY**.

I WAS **CALLED, YOU SEE**-
TO REVEAL GOD'S HOLY MESSAGE TO THOSE WHOM HE HAS **PLACED BEFORE ME**.

FOR, HIS HOLY **CALL, YOU SEE**-
LED HIS NEEDY **CHILDREN TO ME**.

HOLY, HOLY, HOLY-
IS THE CALL OF GOD ALMIGHTY!!!

    LISTEN. LISTEN. LISTEN.

ALMIGHTY GOD SPEAKING TO EARTH'S RESIDENTS

LISTEN. LISTEN. LISTEN.
LISTEN FOR YOU NAME, **O BLESSED CHILDREN**.

FOR, I WILL **CALL, YOU SEE**-
THE NAMES OF THOSE WHO **BELONG TO ME**.

I WILL CALL THE MEEK AND **THE RIGHTEOUS**-
FOR, THEY LONG TO SEE THE FOREVER-**LIVING CHRIST JESUS**.

The Royal Union

I WILL CALL **THE NOBLE ONES-**
FOR, THEY TOO, ARE MY **WORTHY DAUGHTERS AND SONS.**

I WILL CALL **THE MEEK-**
FOR, THEY ARE THE VALUABLE SOULS THAT MY BLESSED SPIRITUAL **REALM DOES SEEK.**

I WILL CALL: I WILL CALL-
I WILL CALL MY LOVELY CHILDREN, SO THAT THEIR BLESSED SOULS **WILL NOT FALL.**

FOR, I, THE LORD **GOD, YOU SEE-**
TRULY LOVE AND ADORE THE CHILDREN WHO **BELONG TO HOLY ME.**

HOLY, HOLY, HOLY-
ARE THE FAITHFUL CHILDREN OF GOD ALMIGHTY!!!

THE MEEK-
ARE THE SERVANTS **WHOM I SEEK.**

FOR, I **DESIRE, YOU SEE-**
FOR THE MEEK ONES TO SERVE THEIR FELLOW **SERVANTS AND ME.**

FOR, **HOLY AND TRUE-**

IS THE GOD WHO WILL ALSO SERVE **BLESSED OBEDIENT YOU.**

HOLY, HOLY, HOLY-
ARE THEY WHO SERVE THE NEEDY CHILDREN OF GOD ALMIGHTY!!!

DEAR CHILDREN: DID YOU HEAR **MY HOLY CALL?**
DID YOU HEAR THE NAMES OF THOSE WHOM **I REFUSE TO LET FALL?**

FOR, **YOUR OBEDIENCE-**
HAS PLACED YOUR SOULS IN **MY HOLY PRESENCE.**

FOR, HOLY ARE THE **NAMES, YOU SEE-**
THAT ARE CALLED BY **GOD, THE ALMIGHTY.**

LISTEN. LISTEN. LISTEN.
LISTEN FOR THE NAMES OF **MY WORTHY CHILDREN.**

FOR, YOUR **FAITHFULNESS-**
HAS OPENED THE DOOR TO MY REALM OF **HOLINESS AND GOODNESS.**

HOLY, HOLY, HOLY-
ARE THE FAITHFUL LOVED ONES OF GOD ALMIGHTY!!!

YOUR WORTHY NAME HAS BEEN **CALLED BY ME-**

The Royal Union

IT HAS BEEN CALLED BY THE REALM OF **SWEET REALITY.**

FOR, **HOLY AND REAL-**
IS THE GOD WHOM YOUR BLESSED SPIRIT CAN **SEE AND FEEL.**

HOLY, HOLY, HOLY-
IS THE REALM OF SWEET REALITY!!!

THE HOLY CALL HAS BEEN SENT **OUT, YOU SEE-**
TO THE WORTHY ONES WHO WERE **CHOSEN BY ME.**

FOR, IN HUMAN **LIFE, YOU SEE-**
YOU SERVED YOUR **LORD GOD FAITHFULLY.**

AND NOW, **DEAR ONES-**
YOU HAVE EARNED THE WONDERFUL TITLE OF BEING **MY CHOSEN DAUGHTERS AND SONS.**

FOR, **HOLY AND TRUE-**
IS THE GOD WHO **CHOSE BLESSED YOU.**

LISTEN, DEAR CHILDREN. **LISTEN TO THE URGENCY-**
FOR, YOUR REALM OF REPENTANCE **IS AN EMERGENCY.**

FOR, ALMIGHTY **GOD, YOU SEE-**

HAS CALLED YOUR SOULS INTO **SWEET REALITY.**

YOU MUST HURRY! YOU MUST HURRY!
FOR, YOUR DEAR SOULS MUST **FACE DIVINE REALITY!!!**

FOR, IT IS **URGENT, YOU SEE-**
THAT YOUR SOULS MAKE PEACE WITH **CHRIST ALMIGHTY.**

FOR, IT IS **A DIVINE NECESSITY-**
THAT YOUR SOULS REPENT TODAY IN THE LIFE-SAVING **PRESENCE OF GOD ALMIGHTY.**

FOR, **HOLY, YOU SEE-**
ARE THE **URGENCY AND EMERGENCY.**

FOR, YOU MUST ASK GOD FOR **FORGIVENESS-**
IF YOU DESIRE TO ENJOY HIS OPEN **REALM OF HOLINESS.**

FOR, **HOLY AND TRUE-**
IS THE GOD WHO IS CALLING **REPENTANT YOU.**

HOLY, HOLY, HOLY-
IS THE GREAT CALL OF GOD ALMIGHTY!!!

The Royal Union

BOOK # NINE

THE URGENCY

THE URGENCY

SUBTITLE

AN EMERGENCY

BY:

BARBARA ANN MARY MACK

BEGAN: OCTOBER 29, 2024

COMPLETED: NOVEMBER 7, 2024

CAN YOU FEEL THE URGENCY, DEAR CHILDREN?

ALMIGHTY GOD SPEAKING TO EARTH'S RESIDENTS TODAY

DEAR CHILDREN-
YES! YOU WHO ARE **MY GREATEST CREATION.**

I WANT YOU- YES! I WANT **ALL OF YOU TO LISTEN.**
YES, DEAR ONES! I AM SPEAKING TO YOU FROM **EVERY NATION.**

FOR, WHAT I AM ABOUT TO SAY TO YOU IS VERY IMPORTANT AND CRUCIAL, IN REGARDS TO WHERE YOU WILL SPEND **SWEET ETERNITY.**
WILL IT BE WITH ME; **THE ALMIGHTY?**

LISTEN TO ME-
FOR IT IS OF **THE UTMOST URGENCY.**

LISTEN TO ME-
FOR, IT IS TRULY **AN EMERGENCY!**

FOR, I, YOUR LORD AND GOD, WANT YOU TO PAY **VERY CLOSE ATTENTION.**

YES, DEAR CHILDREN. I WANT YOU TO STOP WHATEVER YOU ARE THINKING AND DOING, AND PAY CLOSE ATTENTION. FOR, YOU ARE **MY VALUABLE CREATION.**

I AM THE REALM **OF EXISTENCE-**
AND, BEHOLD, DEAR ONES! YOU ARE IN **MY HOLY PRESENCE.**

YOU MUST HEED **MY LAST WARNING-**
FOR, THIS IS AN EMERGENCY, AND YOU MUST SURRENDER YOUR SOULS TO **CHRIST, THE GREAT JUDGE AND KING.**

FOR, HOLY **AND TRUE-**
IS THE GOD WHO WILL **JUDGE ALL OF YOU.**

LISTEN TO ME, AND **YOU WILL SEE-**
THAT YOUR WAY OF LIVING WILL **NOT SET YOUR SOUL FREE.**

HURRY! HURRY! HURRY!
HURRY, DEAR CHILDREN, AND YOU WILL **SEE; THE URGENCY!**

RUN TO ME-
FOR, THIS IS **AN EMERGENCY!**

HURRY! HURRY! **HURRY, O BLESSED ONES!**
COME, AND ENTER THE REALM THAT WELCOMES **MY REPENTANT DAUGHTERS AND SONS.**

HURRY, BEFORE **IT IS TOO LATE!**
HURRY! BEFORE MY HOLY ANGELS **SHUT HEAVEN'S OPEN GATE!!!**

I AM STANDING **AT THE DOOR-**
HURRY! BEFORE MY HOLY PRESENCE AND SPIRIT **STAND NO MORE!**

HURRY! HURRY! HURRY!
FLEE INTO THE OPEN ARMS OF **CHRIST JESUS, THE ALMIGHTY!!!**

DEAR CHILDREN: IT IS **URGENT, YOU SEE-**
THAT YOU BECOME **UNITED WITH ME.**

FOR, **SATAN-**
DESIRES TO STEAL THE VULNERABLE SOULS OF **EVERY WOMAN AND MAN.**

BEWARE! BEWARE! BEWARE!
BEWARE OF THE EVIL REALM THAT **DOESN'T CARE!**

FOR, HE **LURKS, YOU SEE-**

The Royal Union

IN THE MIDST OF THE LOVED ONES WHO **BELONG TO HOLY ME.**

SATAN AND HIS DECEITFUL **FOLLOWERS STEAL-**
FROM THE HOLY GOD **WHO IS ETERNAL, LOVING, AND REAL.**

HE, SATAN, **DENIES-**
FOR, HE IS THE FATHER AND ORIGIN OF **THIEVERY AND LIES.**

HIS REALM **IS REAL-**
AND, HIS LOWLY SERVANTS HAVE COME TO **ROB AND STEAL.**

FOR, HE **DOES DESIRE-**
TO WITNESS MY CHILDREN'S DESTRUCTION IN **HELL'S UNENDING FIRE.**

DEAR CHILDREN-
YES! EVERY **EXISTING NATION.**

BE AWARE! BE AWARE! BE AWARE!
BE AWARE, DEAR CHILDREN, OF SATAN, THE HELL BOUND ONE, **WHO DOESN'T CARE!!!**

FOR, HIS REALM OF UNENDING **SUFFERING AND DESTRUCTION-**

SLYLY LURES MY **UNSUSPECTING CHILDREN.**

FOR, UNHOLY, **BUT TRUE-**
IS THE REALM OF EVIL THAT TRIES VERY HARD TO **STEAL HEAVEN BOUND YOU.**

THEREFORE, DEAR CHILDREN, WHO DESIRE TO FOLLOW LIFE **REWARDING HOLY ME-**
REMEMBER, THAT YOU **MUST LIVE HOLY.**

DEAR CHILDREN: IT IS **URGENT, YOU SEE-**
THAT YOU BECOME **UNITED WITH LIFE-GIVING ME.**

FOR, **SATAN-**
DESIRES TO STEAL THE VULNERABLE SOULS OF THE **LIFE SEEKING WOMAN AND MAN.**

REMEMBER THAT YOUR LIFE CHANGING SITUATION, **YOU SEE-**
IS **AN EMERGENCY.**

REPENT IN THE HOLY PRESENCE OF **HE WHO CAN SAVE-**
FOR, CHRIST JESUS, CAN SAVE THE WEAK ONES **AND THE BRAVE.**

FOR, **HOLY, YOU SEE-**

IS THE GOD WHO HAS COME TO RESCUE THE SINKING SOULS THAT BELONG TO **THE LOVED ONES OF GOD ALMIGHTY.**

**HOLY, HOLY, HOLY-
ARE THE RESCUING HANDS OF GOD ALMIGHTY!!!**

DEAR CHILDREN: **REMEMBER MY PLEA-**
REMEMBER **LIFE SAVING ME.**

FOR, YOU MUST **MOVE IN A HURRY-**
FOR, SATAN AND HIS SERVANTS SLITHER IN THE MIDST OF THE UNSUSPECTING ONES WHO **DESIRE TO BE FREE.**

HE SLITHERS, AND **HE MOVES SLOW-**
FOR, HE FOLLOWS MY VULNERABLE EARTHLY CREATION **WHEREVER THEY GO.**

THEREFORE, YOU MUST MOVE **SWIFTLY, DEAR CHILDREN-**
SO THAT YOU MAY OUT RUN THE REALM OF **UNENDING DESTRUCTION.**

FOR, SATAN **IS CUNNING-**
HE IS THE ENEMY OF CHRIST **JESUS, THE LIFE-SAVING GOD AND KING.**

DEAR CHILDREN: **MOVE VERY FAST-**
SO THAT HIS EVIL PRESENCE WILL **REMAIN IN YOUR PAST.**

FOR, **HOLY, YOU SEE-**
IS THE GOD WHO HAS WARNED YOU ABOUT **SATAN, MY ENEMY.**

FOR, **UNHOLY-**
IS THE **ENEMY OF GOD ALMIGHTY.**

MOVE! MOVE! **MOVE, O BLESSED CHILDREN.**
TRY TO OUT RUN THE REALM OF **EVERLASTING DESTRUCTION!!!**

HOLY, HOLY, HOLY-
IS THE LIFE SAVING CHRIST ALMIGHTY!!!

BOOK # TEN

SALVATION

SALVATION

SUBTITLE

REPENTANCE

BY:

BARBARA ANN MARY MACK

BEGAN: OCTOBER 29, 2024

COMPLETED: NOVEMBER 8, 2024

SALVATION, SALVATION; SWEET, SWEET, SALVATION

ALMIGHTY GOD, THE SAVIOR, SPEAKING TO EARTH'S NEEDY RESIDENTS TODAY

SWEET, SWEET, SALVATION.
IS OFFERED TO **EVERY BLESSED NATION.**

FOR, I, THE LORD JESUS, HAVE **COME BACK, YOU SEE-**
TO OFFER THE GIFT OF SALVATION THAT **COMES FROM DIVINE ROYAL ME.**

FOR, SALVATION IS THE GIFT OF **EVERLASTING LIFE-**
THAT I OFFER TO EVERY **HOLY LIVING HUSBAND AND WIFE.**

SALVATION IS A **DIVINE GIFT, YOU SEE-**
THAT COMES FROM **THE ETERNAL GOD ALMIGHTY.**

DEAR CHILDREN: LIVING A **HOLY AND SIN FREE LIFE-**
WILL REMOVE YOUR SOUL **FROM FUTURE STRIFE.**

WALK WITH ME DURING **THIS TRAGIC JOURNEY-**
SO THAT YOU MAY BE INVITED TO THE HEAVENLY HOME OF **GOD ALMIGHTY.**

WALK WITH YOUR **LOVING SAVIOR-**
AS YOU HEAD IN THE DIRECTION OF GREETING **GOD,**
YOUR HEAVENLY FATHER.

FOR, **HOLY AND TRUE-**
IS THE GOD AND FATHER WHO WILL **WELCOME BLESSED OBEDIENT YOU.**

COME, COME; COME!
ENTER, O REPENTANT ONE: **ENTER MY HEAVENLY KINGDOM.**

FOR, WHERE **I LIVE-**
THERE IS SO MUCH TO **SEE AND GIVE.**

YOU ARE **INVITED BY ME-**
TO ENTER THE GATES THAT LEAD TO THE HEAVENLY HOME OF **THE BLESSED ROYAL TRINITY.**

FOR, **HOLY AND TRUE-**
IS THE HEAVENLY HOME THAT **WELCOMES MY CHOSEN FEW.**

HOLY, HOLY, HOLY-
ARE THE WELCOMED GUESTS OF CHRIST ALMIGHTY!!!

DEAR **CHILDREN-**
LISTEN. LISTEN. LISTEN.

Barbara Ann Mary Mack

FOR, I, YOUR LORD **AND GOD TODAY-**
OFFER YOU THE PATH THAT LEADS TO **MY LIFE REWARDING HOLY WAY.**

I OFFER YOU **SWEET SALVATION-**
THAT I HAVE MADE AVAILABLE TO EVERY **SPIRITUALLY PROSPEROUS NATION.**

I WILL **RELEASE, YOU SEE-**
THE ROAD THAT LEADS TO THE SWEET SALVATION THAT COMES FROM **HOLY ETERNAL ME.**

I WILL **RELEASE-**
THE HEAVENLY REALM THAT GIVES MY EARTHLY LOVED ONES **DIVINE SECURITY AND PEACE.**

SALVATION, SALVATION; **SWEET SALVATION-**
IS GIVEN TO MY OBEDIENT ONES FROM **EVERY EARTHLY NATION.**

IT IS **GIVEN, YOU SEE-**
TO THOSE WHO ARE **FAITHFUL TO HOLY ME.**

FOR, THE ROAD THAT LEADS TO **EVERLASTING LIFE-**
WAS PREPARED BY ALMIGHTY GOD, FOR HIS FAITHFUL EARTHLY SON AND **HIS LOVING WIFE.**

HOLY, HOLY, HOLY-

The Royal Union

IS THE ROAD THAT LEADS TO SWEET SALVATION AND ME!!!

ON THE NARROW ROAD TO SWEET SALVATION

BARBARA SPEAKING

ON THE NARROW ROAD TO **SWEET SALVATION**-
I WILL JOIN THE GOD WHO CREATED HIS LOVED ONES **FROM EVERY NATION.**

I WILL JOIN THE MIGHTY **GOD OF HOPE**-
FOR, HE HELPS HIS WEARY **LOVED ONES TO COPE.**

I WILL **GIVE PRAISE**-
TO MY LIFE-SAVING GOD DURING THESE **BLESSED AND HOLY DAYS.**

I WILL BOW IN **HIS HOLY PRESENCE**-
AS I GREET HIM WITH **DIVINE REVERENCE.**

FOR, **HOLY, YOU SEE**-
IS THE GOD WHO OFFERS **SWEET SALVATION TO ME.**

FOR, ON HIS CROSS OF DIVINE **LOVE, YOU SEE**-
HE SACRIFICED HIS HOLY LIFE FOR THE GREAT CREATION **OF GOD ALMIGHTY.**

FOR, **HOLY AND TRUE**-

IS THE GOD WHO **SAVES ME AND YOU.**

HOLY, HOLY, HOLY-
IS THE SALVATION THAT COMES FROM CHRIST JESUS, THE ALMIGHTY!!!

FOR, CHRIST **JESUS DOES SAVE-**
THOSE WHO HAVE **ENTERED THEIR EARTHLY GRAVE.**

HOLY, HOLY, HOLY-
IS THE LIFE-SAVING GOD ALMIGHTY!!!

SALVATION, SALVATION; **SWEET EVERLASTING SALVATION-**
IT IS A GIFT OF HEAVENLY LOVE THAT IS OFFERED TO THOSE **FROM EVERY NATION.**

IT IS A GIFT OF **EVERLASTING LIFE-**
THAT IS OFFERED TO THE BELIEVING ONE AND HIS **GRATEFUL LOVING WIFE.**

IT IS THE GIFT OF **LIFE EVERLASTING-**
THAT IS GIVEN TO US FROM CHRIST JESUS, OUR **VICTORIOUS SACRIFICED KING.**

HOLY, HOLY, HOLY-
IS CHRIST JESUS' GIFT OF SALVATION-

FOR, IT IS OFFERED TO HIS BELIEVING GREAT CREATION.

ENTER MY GIFT OF DIVINE SALVATION, SAYS THE LORD GOD

CHRIST JESUS, OUR SAVING ROYAL GOD, SPEAKING TO EARTH'S RESIDENTS TODAY

ENTER MY GIFT OF **DIVINE SALVATION-**
FOR, I OFFER IT TO MY LITTLE ONES **FROM EVERY NATION.**

IT IS **LIFE REWARDING-**
FOR, IT IS A DIVINE GIFT FROM CHRIST JESUS, YOUR HEAVEN SENT **GOD AND KING.**

HOLY, HOLY, HOLY-
IS THE HEAVENLY GIFT OF EVERLASTING LIFE THAT COMES FROM GOD ALMIGHTY!!!

ENJOY MY HEAVENLY GIFT, **DEAR LITTLE CHILDREN-**
FOR, I TRULY LOVE AND ADORE **MY GREATEST CREATION.**

BARBARA SPEAKING TO GOD'S EARTHLY LOVED ONES TODAY

SALVATION, SALVATION; SWEET, SWEET, SALVATION.
IT IS THE GIFT OF LOVE THAT THE LORD SACRIFICED FOR **HIS GREAT CREATION.**

FOR, **HOLY AND TRUE-**
IS THE DEPTH OF DIVINE LOVE THAT CHRIST JESUS HAS FOR **ME AND WORTHY YOU.**

CHRIST JESUS' REALM OF SALVATION

BARBARA SPEAKING TO EARTH'S RESIDENTS TODAY

CHRIST JESUS' REALM OF SALVATION HAS CAPTURED **GOD'S CHOSEN FEW.**
IT HAS CAPTURED ME AND **BLESSED YOU.**

FOR, JESUS' REALM OF **HOPE AND MERCY-**
PAVED THE WAY FOR THE REPENT ONES WHO SOUGHT **THE HOLY SPIRIT OF GOD ALMIGHTY.**

REJOICE, O SWEET **REPENTANT ONE!**
REJOICE IN THE HOLY PRESENCE OF GOD, THE FATHER'S, **ONLY BEGOTTEN SON!**

FOR, HE IS **THE DIVINE SAVIOR-**
WHO CALLS AND INVITES HIS **WORTHY SON AND DAUGHTER.**

The Royal Union

FOR, **HOLY, YOU SEE-**
IS THE GOD WHO OFFERS THE VALUABLE GIFT OF SWEET SALVATION TO **THE BLESSED ONES AND ME.**

**HOLY, HOLY, HOLY-
IS THE ROAD THAT LEADS TO HEAVENLY ECSTASY!!!**

REJOICE, O BLESSED SAVED ONES, **REJOICE!**
UNITE YOUR HOLY TUNES AS **ONE UNIFIED VOICE!**

REJOICE IN THE LAND OF SWEET SALVATION **AND THE LIVING!**
REJOICE, AS ONE VOICE, IN THE HOLY PRESENCE OF **CHRIST JESUS, THE FOREVER-LIVING KING!**

FOR, **HOLY, YOU SEE-**
IS CHRIST JESUS, THE LIFE-**SAVING KING ALMIGHTY.**

WAKE UP! WAKE UP! WAKE UP!!!

BARBARA SPEAKING TO EARTH'S RESIDENTS TODAY

WAKE UP! WAKE UP! **WAKE UP, EVERY BLESSED NATION!**
WAKE UP, ALL YOU LANDS! FOR, YOU ARE IN THE PRESENCE OF **THE FOREVER-LIVING KING AND GOD OF SWEET SALVATION!**

WAKE UP, YOU **LONELY HILL!**
FOR, IT IS TIME FOR EVERYONE TO **HONOR GOD'S HOLY WILL!**

WAKE UP **ALL YOU LANDS!**
DO YOU NOT KNOW THAT YOU ARE GOVERNED BY **THE POWER OF GOD'S MIGHTY HANDS?**

WAKE UP, YOU **FLOWING RIVERS!**
OPEN THE EARS OF GOD'S LISTENING **SONS AND DAUGHTERS!**

FOR, HE HAS **ARRIVED, YOU SEE-**
IN THE MIDST OF **THIS WORLD'S TRAGEDY.**

CHRIST JESUS, THE FOREVER-LIVING SAVING GOD SPEAKING

FOR, I, THE LORD **JESUS, YOU SEE-**
HAVE RETURNED, SO THAT I MAY LEAD YOU AWAY FROM **EARTH'S IMPENDING DESTRUCTION AND TRAGEDY.**

FLEE! FLEE! FLEE!!!
FLEE INTO THE WAITING ARMS OF **CHRIST JESUS, THE ALMIGHTY!!!**

FOR, I WANT **YOU TO KNOW-**

THAT THE WORLD'S TRAGEDIES WILL FOLLOW YOU **WHEREVER YOU GO.**

THEREFORE, **LITTLE ONES-**
I AM SPEAKING TO ALL OF MY EARTHLY **DAUGHTERS AND SONS.**

BECAUSE, YOU ARE A PART OF **THIS PASSING WORLD-**
SATAN WILL TRY TO DISCOURAGE AND SINK EVERY **SPIRITUALLY UNPROTECTED LITTLE BOY AND GIRL.**

YOU MUST HEAD IN **THE DIRECTION-**
OF THE KING AND GOD OF **EVERLASTING SALVATION.**

FOR, IT IS ONLY A MATTER OF **TIME, YOU SEE-**
THAT THIS WORLD WILL PASS IN THE MIDST OF **SATAN'S TRAGEDY.**

HURRY! HURRY! HURRY!
PRESERVE A SEAT THAT **LEADS TO GOD ALMIGHTY!**

DO NOT **LINGER!**
FOR, SATAN IS POINTING **HIS DESTRUCTIVE FINGER!**

HURRY! HURRY! HURRY, O FLEEING ONES!

Barbara Ann Mary Mack

HURRY TO ME, SO THAT SATAN WILL NOT TAKE DOWN AND CAPTURE **MY VULNERABLE DAUGHTERS AND SONS!**

FLEE! FLEE! FLEE!
REMOVE YOUR VULNERABLE PRESENCE FROM **THIS PASSING WORLD'S ULTIMATE TRAGEDY!**

FOR, **I ALONE, YOU SEE-**
CAN RESCUE AND SAVE **THOSE WHO COME TO ME.**

HURRY! HURRY! HURRY!
ENTER THE REALM THAT HOUSES **CHRIST JESUS, THE ALMIGHTY!!!**

DO NOT WAIT-
HURRY, DEAR CHILDREN, BEFORE **IT IS TOO LATE!!!**

FOR, IN A MATTER OF **SECONDS, YOU SEE-**
YOU MAY BECOME A PART OF THIS PASSING **WORLD'S ULTIMATE TRAGEDY.**

LEAN TOWARDS **MY HOLY WAY-**
HURRY! HURRY! HURR**Y, AND ENTER ME TODAY!!!**

FOR, **UNHOLY, BUT REAL-**
IS SATAN, WHO HAS **COME TO STEAL!!!**

The Royal Union

LEAVE **BEHIND YOU-**
EVERYTHING THAT IS **UNHOLY AND UNTRUE.**

HURRY! HURRY! HURRY!
ENTER THE OPEN ARMS THAT BELONG TO THE KING OF SALVATION; **CHRIST JESUS, THE ROYAL ALMIGHTY!!!**

BOOK # ELEVEN

MY TREASURE

MY TREASURE: MY GOD

SUBTITLE:

MY GIFT OF FINE GOLD

BY;

BARBARA ANN MARY MACK

BEGAN: OCTOBER 29, 2024

COMPLETED: NOVEMBER 8, 2024

MY TREASURE; MY HOLY TREASURE: ALMIGHTY GOD

BARBARA SPEAKING

MY TREASURE; **MY HOLY TREASURE-**
THE GOD WHO GIVES ME **SPIRITUAL PLEASURE.**

OH, WHAT AN IMMENSE AMOUNT OF **WEALTH, YOU SEE-**
HE IS THE WEALTH THAT TRULY SATISFIES HIS DEVOTED **LOVED ONES AND ME.**

HE IS THE POT OF TREASURE THAT DESCENDED FROM **SWEET HEAVEN TO ME-**
FOR, HE IS THE ALL-POWERFUL AND ALL-PRESENT **CHRIST JESUS, THE ALMIGHTY.**

OH, WHAT A DIVINE **PROFITABLE JOY-**
TO HAVE AND HOLD A HEAVEN SENT BASKET OF WEALTH THAT CANNOT BE TAKEN AWAY **NOR, SATAN CAN DESTROY.**

HOLY IS MY **DESCENDED TREASURE-**
HE IS A WEALTH THAT NO ONE CAN **COMPARE WITH NOR MEASURE.**

FOR, **HE IS MINE-**
UNTIL THE REALM OF **NEVER ENDING TIME.**

FOR, HE IS. HE IS. **HE IS, YOU SEE-**
THE HEAVEN SENT TREASURE THAT **DESCENDED TO ME.**

FOR, **GOD ALMIGHTY-**
IS THE VALUABLE TREASURE THAT DESCENDED TO HIS EARTHLY **LOVED ONES AND ME.**

HOLY AND ETERNAL **IS THE TREASURE-**
THAT GIVES EARTH'S NEEDY LOVED ONES UNENDING **SPIRITUAL DELIGHTFUL PLEASURE.**

HE IS THE GIFT THAT EXCITES MY **OBEDIENT SOUL DAILY.**
FOR, HE IS THE **ETERNAL GOD ALMIGHTY.**

HE IS **THE FAITHFUL ONE-**
HE IS CHRIST JESUS, GOD, THE FATHER'S, **ONLY BEGOTTEN SON.**

FOR, HE, **ALONE, YOU SEE-**
WAS CALLED INTO EXISTENCE BY **GOD, OUR FATHER, ALMIGHTY.**

HOLY IS **HIS EXISTENCE-**

ETERNAL IS **HIS HOLY PRESENCE.**

I HAVE A DIVINE HEAVEN SENT **TREASURE BOX, YOU SEE-**
THAT DESCENDED **ONLY TO ME.**

FOR, GOD **ALMIGHTY, YOU SEE-**
IS THE TREASURE WHO HAS DESCENDED TO HIS BELIEVING **LOVED ONES AND FAITHFUL ME.**

I WILL NOT **BURY, YOU SEE-**
THE HEAVEN SENT TREASURE THAT WAS GIVEN TO **BLESSED TRUSTING ME.**

HOLY, HOLY, HOLY-
IS THE TREASURE THAT DESCENDED TO **WORTHY ME!!!**

MY TREASURE IS PURE, **ETERNAL, AND REAL.**
HE IS A GIFT OF LOVE THAT **NO ONE CAN STEAL.**

FOR, **HOLY, YOU SEE-**
IS THE TREASURE AND GIFT OF LOVE **CALLED GOD ALMIGHTY.**

I WILL SHOW **OFF, YOU SEE-**
THE HOLY GIFT THAT **DESCENDED TO ME.**

The Royal Union

FOR, I WANT THE WORLD TO **SEE AND KNOW-**
THAT MY DIVINE TREASURE TRAVELS WITH ME WHEREVER **MY BODY AND SOUL GO.**

HOLY IS MY **ROYAL TREASURE-**
HIS DIVINE ORIGIN GIVES US BELIEVING ONES **JOYFUL PLEASURE.**

FOR, HIS IS **A LOVE-**
THAT MOVES IN THE MIDST OF **SWEET PARADISE ABOVE.**

HE GIVES ME **SPIRITUAL DELIGHT-**
WHENEVER HE EXHIBITS **HIS GREAT MIGHT.**

FOR, **HOLY AND TRUE-**
IS THE TREASURE THAT DESCENDED TO **ME AND YOU.**

HOLY, HOLY, HOLY-
IS MY VALUABLE GIFT AND TREASURE CALLED CHRIST JESUS, THE ALMIGHTY!!!

FOR, HIS **EXISTENCE IS REAL-**
HIS IS AN EXPERIENCE THAT THE FAITHFUL AND OBEDIENT ONES **CAN SURELY SEE AND FEEL.**

FOR, **HOLY AND TRUE-**

IS THE TREASURE THAT IS OFFERED TO **BLESSED ME AND YOU.**

HOLY, HOLY, HOLINESS-
MOVES IN THE MIDST OF ALMIGHTY GOD'S **ROYALTY AND GOODNESS.**

HIS **DIVINE MERCY-**
TRANSCENDS THE WORLD OF **DECEIT AND TRICKERY.**

FOR, **HOLY, YOU SEE-**
IS THE POT OF TREASURED LOVE **CALLED, MY GOD ALMIGHTY.**

FOR, **HOLY, YOU SEE-**
IS THE VALUABLE ROYAL TREASURE THAT **DESCENDED TO BLESSED ME.**

HOLY, HOLY, HOLY-
IS MY UNFOLDING TREASURE CALLED CHRIST JESUS, THE ALMIGHTY!!!

I WILL NOT **BURY, YOU SEE-**
THE HEAVEN DESCENDED TREASURE THAT WAS GIVEN TO ME.

FOR, THE TREASURE THAT I HOLD VERY **CLOSE TO MY HEART-**

The Royal Union

IS A DIVINE TREASURE THAT I WILL NEVER PART.

FOR, THE **TREASURE, YOU SEE-**
IS THE PRESENCE AND HOLY **SPIRIT OF GOD ALMIGHTY.**

I WILL NOT BURY THE GIFT THAT IS **A VALUABLE PART OF ME.**
FOR, THAT HOLY GIFT IS THE ETERNAL SPIRIT OF **GOD, THE ALMIGHTY.**

OH, MY HEART AND SPIRIT REJOICE **THROUGHOUT EACH DAY-**
AS MY TREASURE AND I LEAD HIS LOVED ONES TO **HIS HOLY LIFE-SAVING AND REWARDING WAY.**

FOR, MY HOLY **TREASURE, YOU SEE-**
REVEALS HIS LOVE FOR **HIS BLESSED LITTLE ONES AND ME.**

HOLY, HOLY, HOLY-
IS THE TREASURE CALLED GOD ALMIGHTY!!!

BARBARA SPEAKING TO ALMIGHTY GOD, HER HEAVEN DESCENDED TREASURE

DEAR HOLY **TREASURE OF MINE-**

I AM TRULY GRATEFUL THAT YOU HAVE CHOSEN TO BE WITH YOUR EARTHLY LOVED ONES AND ME DURING **THIS TRAGIC PERIOD OF TIME.**

FOR, YOU **DID RELIEVE-**
EVERY DISCOMFORT THAT MY WANDERING **SPIRIT DID RECEIVE.**

YOU ALONE, O BLESSED **TREASURE OF MINE-**
ARE TRULY **ONE OF A KIND.**

BOOK # TWELVE

YOURS

YOURS

BY:

BARBARA ANN MARY MACK

BEGAN: OCTOBER 29, 2024

COMPLETED NOVEMBER 8, 2024

INTRODUCTION

ETERNITY; SWEET EXISTING ETERNITY, HAS CAPTURED BLESSED ME

<u>BARBARA SPEAKING TO ALMIGHTY GOD; SWEET ETERNITY</u>

OH SWEET **LONGED FOR ETERNITY-**
YOU HAVE CAPTURED THE MIND, BODY, AND SOUL THAT BELONG TO **OBEDIENT AND GRATEFUL ME.**

YOU HAVE **CAPTURED THE DAUGHTER-**
WHO GIVES CONTINUOUS PRAISE TO ALMIGHTY GOD, HER **FOREVER-LIVING HEAVENLY FATHER.**

YOU HAVE **CAPTURE ME-**
WITH THE WONDERFUL BLESSINGS THAT DESCENDED FROM THE **THRONE OF GOD, THE FATHER, ALMIGHTY.**

I AM **COMPLETELY-**
DEVOTED TO THE HOLY GOD WHO TRULY LOVES HIS **GREAT CREATION AND ME.**

I AM YOURS, **OH HEAVENLY ONE.**
I AM A TRUE SERVANT OF CHRIST JESUS, YOUR **FAITHFUL ONLY BEGOTTEN SON.**

I AM YOURS THROUGHOUT THE REALM OF **UNENDING TIME.**
I WILL FOREVER FOLLOW YOUR HOLY WAY, **FOR YOU ARE MINE.**

HOLY, HOLY, HOLY-
IS MY HEAVEN SENT TREASURE ALMIGHTY!!!

ALMIGHTY GOD, THE HOLY ONE, HAS COMPLETE OWNERSHIP OVER ME

BARBARA SPEAKING TO ALMIGHTY GOD, THE FATHER

MY GOD: IN THE MIDDLE OF THE NIGHT, **I AM YOURS.** THROUGHOUT THE DAY, YOU OPEN IN MY GRATEFUL PRESENCE, **YOUR LIFE-SAVING DOORS.**

I AM YOURS THROUGHOUT **EACH DAY-**
I AM YOURS, O HOLY MASTER AND GOD, WHENEVER MY SPIRITUALLY **WEAK KNEES BEND AS I PRAY.**

I AM YOURS EACH AND **EVERY MORNING.**
FOR, I AM ONE OF CHRIST JESUS' GREATEST CREATIONS; AND HE IS **MY ROYAL GOD AND KING.**

FOR, **HOLY AND TRUE-**
IS THE LOVE AND GOD WHO MADE A GREAT SACRIFICE FOR YOUR EARTHLY LOVED ONES AND ME; **AS HE HONORED YOU.**

BARBARA SPEAKING

HOLY, HOLY, HOLY-
IS THE LOVE THAT I HAVE FOR **GOD, THE ALMIGHTY!!!**

FOR, HIS **LOVE, YOU SEE-**
SUSTAINS **GRATEFUL ME.**

I AM THE EPITOME OF MY GOD'S UNENDING REALM OF **DIVINE LOVE-**
THAT DESCENDED TO ME FROM **SWEET HEAVEN ABOVE.**

FOR, **HOLY, YOU SEE-**
ARE THE MANY EXPRESSIONS OF LOVE THAT **HE REVEALS TO ME.**

BARBARA SPEAKING TO ALMIGHTY GOD; CHRIST JESUS, THE FATHER

I AM YOURS DURING, AND THROUGH **MY MOMENTS OF WEAKNESS-**
AS YOU COMFORT ME IN **YOUR REALM OF HOLINESS.**

FOR, MY GRATITUDE, **LORD JESUS-**
IS FOR THE GOD AND CREATOR OF THE WEAK ONES **AND THE RIGHTEOUS.**

HOLY, HOLY, HOLY-

IS MY REALM OF UNENDING LOVE AND DEVOTION TO MY SAVING GOD ALMIGHTY!!!

FOR, **YOU HAVE PROVEN-**
YOUR UNDYING LOVE FOR **YOUR GREATEST CREATION.**

I AM YOURS ALONE, **LORD JESUS-**
I BELONG TO THE HOLY GOD AND SAVIOR OF **THE FAITHFUL ONES AND THE RIGHTEOUS.**

NO ONE CAN **CAPTURE, YOU SEE-**
THE TRUE LOVE THAT BELONGS TO **ALMIGHTY GOD AND ME.**

NO ONE **COULD STEAL-**
A HEAVENLY LOVE THAT IS **DEFINITELY REAL.**

FOR, **HOLY, YOU SEE-**
IS MY DEVOTION TO THE RELATIONSHIP THAT IS SHARED BY **ALMIGHTY GOD AND ME.**

HOLY, HOLY, HOLY-
IS MY COMMITMENT TO GOD ALMIGHTY!!!

FOR, ALL ROADS LEAD TO LIFE IN CHRIST JESUS, OUR LOVING **GOD AND SAVIOR.**

The Royal Union

FOR, THE ORIGIN OF ALL HOLY ROADS COME FROM ALMIGHTY GOD, **OUR ETERNAL FATHER.**

THE NARROW ROAD TO EVERLASTING **LIFE, YOU SEE-** IS CALLED THE FOREVER-**LIVING CHRIST ALMIGHTY.**

FOR, HE IS **THE SALVATION-**
OF EVERY **BLESSED NATION.**

HIS HOLY ROAD GUIDES US AWAY FROM SATAN'S **REALM OF DESTRUCTION.**
AS WE TURN TO THE KING AND GOD OF **SWEET SALVATION.**

REACH FOR IT! REACH FOR IT! REACH FOR THE **GOD AND KING OF SWEET SALVATION.**
REACH FOR CHRIST JESUS, FOR HE IS KING OVER **EVERY BLESSED NATION.**

YOURS; IS THE ROAD **TO RIGHTEOUSNESS-**
YOURS, IS THE REALM OF **GODLY HOLINESS.**

YOURS IS THE ONLY WAY TO **LIFE ETERNAL, YOU SEE-**
FOR, YOURS IS THE LOVE THAT HAS **CAPTURED OBEDIENT ME.**

I WILL FOLLOW **YOUR HOLY WAY-**

I WILL SLEEP WITHIN YOUR **REALM OF A NEW GLORIOUS DAY.**

I WILL WALK IN YOUR HOLY VISIBLE **FOOTSTEPS, YOU SEE-**
FOR, I WANT TO BE LIKE CHRIST **JESUS, THE ALMIGHTY.**

I WILL **LOOK FOR YOU-**
IN EVERY GOOD AND HOLY **THING THAT I DO.**

I WILL FOLLOW, **EVERY DAY-**
YOUR AWESOME **HOLY WAY.**

FOR, YOUR HOLY WAY, **IS THE ONLY WAY-**
THAT WILL LEAD TO **A HAPPIER DAY.**

I WILL FOLLOW YOUR HOLY **LEAD, DEAR GOD-**
AS YOU LEAD ME TO YOUR LAND OF **EVERLASTING LOVE.**

FOR, **HOLY AND TRUE-**
IS THE LOVE THAT I RECEIVE FROM **BLESSED ETERNAL YOU.**

HOLY, HOLY, HOLY-
IS THE LAND OF THE LIVING CALLED GOD ALMIGHTY!!!

AND WHEN CHRIST JESUS, THE FOREVER-LIVING KING, LOOKED UPON MY BLESSED SOUL

BARBARA SPEAKING

AND, WHEN CHRIST JESUS, THE FOREVER-LIVING ROYAL KING, LOOKED UPON MY SOUL IN THE MIDST OF **THE GREAT HEAVENLY MULTITUDE**-
HIS HOLY SPIRIT REVEALED TO ME **HIS DEEPEST GRATITUDE.**

FOR, THE ROYAL KING WAS **TRULY GRATEFUL**-
HIS HOLY SPIRIT REVEALED TO ME THAT THE COMPLETION OF **MY EARTHLY ASSIGNMENT WAS WONDERFUL.**

OH, HOW **GRAND IT IS**-
TO HAVE BEEN AN **EARTHLY MESSENGER OF HIS.**

OH, **HOW GRAND**-
TO BE A PART OF **HIS HEAVENLY BAND.**

FOR, MY SPIRIT DID **REJOICE, YOU SEE**-
IN THE MIDST OF THE HEAVENLY INSTRUMENTS OF **GOD ALMIGHTY.**

THE MUSIC WAS GRAND **AND APPEALING**-

FOR, IT WAS CALLED INTO EXISTENCE BY ALMIGHTY GOD, **THE DIVINE ROYAL KING.**

FOR, **HOLY, YOU SEE-**
IS THE ROYAL GOD WHO **NOTICED BLESSED ME.**

**HOLY, HOLY, HOLY-
IS THE KING'S ROYALTY!!!**

BOOK # THIRTEEN

AMAZING IS HE

AMAZING IS HE

SUBTITLE:

ALMIGHTY GOD

BY:

BARBARA ANN MARY MACK

BEGAN: OCTOBER 29, 2024

COMPLETED: NOVEMBER 9, 2024

INTRODUCTION

THROUGH THE YEARS, THE LORD GOD HAS PERFORMED MANY AMAZING OCCURRENCES IN MY LIFE AND THE LIVES OF MANY INDIVIDUALS. HE HAS PRODUCED MANY MIRACULOUS HAPPENINGS THROUGHOUT THE WORLD. IT'S A WONDER THAT MANY PEOPLE GO UNDER THE LABEL OR TITLE OF BEING AN ATHEIST.

FOR ONE THING: WHERE DID EVERYTHING COME FROM? HOW CAN ONE EXPLAIN THE STABILITY OF THE UNIVERSE AND THE FORMATION AND REPRODUCTION OF PHYSICAL LIFE? ALL OF THESE THINGS, AND MANY OTHER OCCURRENCES AND EXISTING FACTS, GIVE CREDENCE TO THE EXISTENCE OF ALMIGHTY GOD. SOME DO NOT ACCEPT THE VISIBLE AND PHYSICAL FACTS PERTAINING TO DIVINE CREATION. BUT, THEIR BELIEF, OR NON-BELIEF, DOESN'T CHANGE THE FACTS AT ALL. DIVINE CREATION IS A REALITY NOT A DELUSION NOR FAIRYTALE. ALMIGHTY GOD HAS PRODUCED AND CAUSED MANY HAPPENINGS THROUGH EACH GENERATION THAT GAVE CREDENCE TO HIS EXISTENCE AND CONNECTION WITH MANKIND. I AM

A GENUINE WITNESS TO MANY OF THE MIRACULOUS INTERVENTIONS AND MIRACLES THAT COULD ONLY COME FROM A DIVINE HIGHER POWER. THESE OCCURRENCES HAVE REVEALED AND MANIFESTED PHYSICAL AND MATERIAL RESULTS, WHICH PROVED THE REALITY OF GOD'S AMAZING INVOLVEMENT IN OUR LIVES TODAY. THERE ARE NO RATIONAL EXPLANATIONS THAT COULD COMBAT THE REALITY OF DIVINE EXISTENCE IN OUR MIDST. HE IS TRULY AMAZING! HE IS TRULY AMAZING! ALMIGHTY GOD, THE BELOVED TRINITY, IS TRULY AMAZING, FOR HE DOES EXIST TODAY!!!

HOLY, HOLY, HOLY-
IS THE EXISTENCE OF GOD ALMIGHTY!!!

HALLELUJAH!!! ALLELUIA!!!

AMAZING. AMAZING. ALMIGHTY GOD IS TRULY AMAZING

BARBARA SPEAKING

AMAZING! AMAZING!
AMAZING IS CHRIST JESUS, THE FORETOLD EVERLASTING **REIGNING GOD AND KING.**

FOR, HE HAS DONE GREAT AND HOLY WORKS **IN OUR MIDST-**
TO LET THE WORLD KNOW THAT **HE DOES EXIST.**

HE IS THE DIVINE **TRUTH, YOU SEE-**
THAT LEADS HIS EARTHLY LOVED ONES IN THE DIRECTION OF **SWEET TRANQUILITY.**

HE IS THE HEAVEN **SENT RULER-**
AND, HE'S ALMIGHTY GOD, THE SON; AND **OUR LIVING SAVIOR.**

BEHOLD THE **KING OF KINGS-**
WHO DOES GREAT AND **HOLY THINGS.**

FOR, HE IS **THE RIGHTEOUS ONE-**

WHO REIGNS AS GOD, THE FATHER'S, **ONLY BEGOTTEN SON.**

HE IS **THE ROYAL KING-**
HE IS ALMIGHTY **GOD, THE AMAZING!!!**

HE IS GOD, THE FATHER'S, **ONLY BEGOTTEN SON-**
HE IS THE RULER OVER THE RIGHTEOUS ONES; AND,
HE IS ALSO **ALMIGHTY GOD, THE HOLY ONE.**

FOR, **HOLY, YOU SEE-**
IS THE SON WHO WAS BEGOTTEN BY HIS ROYAL FATHER, **THE DIVINE AND HEAVENLY ALMIGHTY.**

FOR, **HOLY AND TRUE-**
IS THE FATHER'S ONLY BEGOTTEN SON WHO SEES **THE BLESSED ONES THROUGH.**

HE IS KING! HE IS KING!
HE, CHRIST JESUS, IS GOD, THE FATHER'S, GREAT REALM OF WONDERS, **WHO IS TRULY AMAZING!**

HOLY, HOLY, HOLY-
IS THE AMAZING GOD ALMIGHTY!!!

FOR, HE **PRESENTS TO US-**
THE AVAILABILITY OF THE HOLY SPIRIT **AND CHRIST JESUS.**

FOR, CHRIST **JESUS, THE HOLY ONE-**
WILL NEVER ABANDON HIS **OBEDIENT DAUGHTER AND SON.**

BARBARA SPEAKING TO CHRIST JESUS, OUR AMAZING HEAVEN SENT GOD

SOOTHE ME, O GREAT AND **HOLY GOD ABOVE.**
SOOTHE MY MIND, BODY, AND SOUL, WITH **YOUR AMAZING LOVE.**

SOOTHE ME IN **THE MORNING-**
AS I REVERE CHRIST JESUS, THE **LIVING ROYAL KING.**

SOOTHE MY BLESSED SOUL IN **THE MID-AFTERNOON-**
FOR, IN SWEET HEAVEN THERE IS **ALWAYS PLENTY OF ROOM.**

SOOTHE MY **NEEDY BEING-**
IN THE **EARLY EVENING.**

SOOTHE ME THROUGHOUT **THE WEARY NIGHT-**
FOR, I KNOW THAT YOUR AMAZING LOVE KEEPS ME WITHIN **YOUR HOLY SIGHT.**

OH HOLY **COMPASSIONATE GOD-**

The Royal Union

I REALLY ENJOY THE BOUNTY OF YOUR SPIRITUAL AND **PHYSICAL DIVINE AMAZING LOVE.**

FOR, I **DESIRE TO KEEP-**
YOUR REALM OF AMAZING LOVE **WHENEVER I SLEEP.**

FOR, **HOLY AND TRUE-**
IS YOUR REALM OF AMAZING LOVE THAT SEES YOUR BLESSED **OBEDIENT ONES THROUGH.**

HOLY, HOLY, HOLY-
IS THE AMAZING LOVE CALLED GOD ALMIGHTY!!!

THE REALM OF DIVINE ROYAL AMAZING LOVE HAS FOLLWED MY BLESSED SPIRIT

BARBARA SPEAKING

THE REALM OF **DIVINE AMAZING LOVE-**
HAS FOLLOWED MY BLESSED SPIRIT FROM **SWEET HEAVEN ABOVE.**

FOR, ALMIGHTY GOD, THE **AMAZING ROYAL ONE-**
HAS GIVEN TO US CHRIST JESUS, HIS **ROYAL ONLY BEGOTTEN SON.**

FOR, **HIS DIVINITY-**

HAS CAPTURED **OBEDIENT ME.**

HOLY, HOLY, HOLY-
IS CHRIST JESUS, THE KING OF DIVINE ROYALTY!!!

FOR, HE LIVES AND **REIGNS, YOU SEE-**
IN THE MIDST OF **BLESSED YOU AND ME.**

HE HAS **CHOSEN, YOU SEE-**
OBEDIENT AND **HUMBLED ME.**

HOLY, HOLY, HOLY-
IS THE KING WHO HAS CHOSEN BLESSED YOU AND ME.

FOR, WE ARE **HIS, YOU SEE-**
WE ARE THE GIFTS THAT WERE GIVEN BY **GOD, THE FATHER, ALMIGHTY.**

FOR, **HOLY AND TRUE-**
IS THE ROYAL KING WHO HAS ACCEPTED THE FATHER'S GENEROUS GIFTS, WHICH ARE **ME AND BLESSED YOU.**

FOR, GOD, THE **FATHER, YOU SEE-**
TRULY LOVES **YOU AND ME.**

HOLY, HOLY, HOLY-
IS GOD, THE FATHER, ALMIGHTY!!!

The Royal Union

BOOK # FOURTEEN

A STRONG LOVE

A STRONG LOVE

BY:

BARBARA ANN MARY MACK

BEGAN: OCTOBER 29, 202

COMPLETED: NOVEMBER 9, 2024

A LOVE THAT IS DIVINE AND SECURE

BARBARA SPEAKING TO ALMIGHTY GOD, THE HEAVEN SENT ROYAL BEGOTTEN SON

MY GOD: OURS IS **A STRONG LOVE-**
THAT DESCENDED FROM **HEAVEN ABOVE.**

IT IS **A PURE LOVE-**
THAT INCLUDES **SWEET HEAVEN ABOVE**

IT IS **VERY STRONG-**
IT IS A UNITY THAT HOLDS US **TOGETHER ALL DAY LONG.**

IT IS **RIGHTEOUS-**
IT WAS CALLED INTO EXISTENCE BY THE HOLY AND MIGHTY **KING JESUS.**

IT IS **A SACRED LOVE-**
THAT MOVES WITHIN THE OPEN GATES OF **SWEET HEAVEN ABOVE.**

IT IS **A SILENT LOVE-**

THAT MOVES WITHOUT A SOUND IN HOLY **HEAVEN ABOVE.**

IT IS A ROYAL LOVE THAT IS KNOWN FOR **ITS DIGNITY.**
FOR, IT WAS CALLED INTO EXISTENCE BY THE ONE AND **ONLY GOD ALMIGHTY.**

FOR, **HOLY, YOU SEE-**
IS THE STRENGTH OF OUR LOVE THAT IS RULED AND GOVERNED **BY GOD, THE ALMIGHTY.**

HIS IS A LOVE THAT HAS CAPTURED MY BLESSED SOUL

BARBARA SPEAKING

A STRONG LOVE HAS **CAPTURED MY BLESSED SOUL-**
A LOVE THAT IS MORE POTENT AND PROFITABLE THAN **EVERY FILLED BASKET OF GOLD.**

A STRONG AND SECURE LOVE THAT HAS CARRIED ME **THROUGH THE YEARS.**
A LOVE THAT HAS CAUGHT **MY MANY FALLEN TEARS.**

I HAVE **FELT THE LOVE-**
THAT HAS GAINED ITS STRENGTH FROM **HEAVEN ABOVE.**

Barbara Ann Mary Mack

FOR, **HOLY, YOU SEE-**
IS THE HEAVEN SENT LOVE THAT GIVES DIVINE STRENGTH AND **COURAGE TO ME.**

IT IS A STRONG AND **OBEDIENT LOVE-**
THAT I SHARE WITH **MY HEAVENLY GOD ABOVE.**

IT REMAINS **WITHIN ME-**
FOR, IT IS A LOVE THAT REVEALS THE HOLY PRESENCE OF **GOD ALMIGHTY.**

HOLY, HOLY, HOLY-
IS THE STRENGTH AND LOVE OF GOD ALMIGHTY!!!

BOOK # FIFTEEN

SOMEONE TO LOVE ME

SOMEONE TO LOVE ME

BY:

BARBARA ANN MARY MACK

BEGAN: OCTOBER 29, 2024

COMPLETED: NOVEMBER 9, 2024

INTRODUCTION

Within the realm of divine love, I have found someone who truly loves me. The love is an unconditional love. It is a love that protects my soul from the realm of evil that lurks in the midst of earth's vulnerable inhabitants. It is a realm of evil that doesn't discriminates. It is a realm that truly hates. It is a realm of destruction that constantly seeks the souls of almighty God's great creation. But, the realm of divine love that sought my needy soul, watches over me and God's earthly loved ones today. I will always treasure and believe in the divine love, for he is truly mine. My blessed soul and spirit bow in the holy presence of almighty God, for he has truly blessed me.

HALLELUJAH!!! ALLELUIA!!! PRAISE THE LORD!!!

SOMEONE TO LOVE ME

BARBARA SPEAKING

I HAVE FOUND-
SOMEONE WHO IS **ALWAYS AROUND.**

FOR, I WANT A LOVE THAT **I CAN FEEL.**
I WANT A LOVE THAT IS **EVERLASTING AND REAL.**

I DID DO SOME **SEARCHING, YOU SEE-**
AND, I FOUND THE PERFECT **LOVE FOR ME.**

IT IS A LOVE THAT I CAN **PLACE MY TRUST IN.**
IT IS A LOVE THAT IS MY VERY **BEST ETERNAL FRIEND.**

FOR, HE IS GENUINE **AND EVERLASTING.**
YES! HE IS CHRIST JESUS, **MY ROYAL GOD AND KING.**

HE IS REAL!
HE IS A LOVE THAT MY BLESSED SPIRIT **CAN SEE AND FEEL.**

HIS IS A **PERMANENT LOVE-**
THAT DESCENDED TO ME FROM **SWEET HEAVEN ABOVE.**

HE IS MY **LIFE'S SOURCE-**
HE IS MY HEAVENLY **DIVINE FORCE.**

FOR, HE **MOVES, YOU SEE-**
IN THE MIDST OF THE **BLESSED ONES AND ME.**

I FOUND A **LOVE, YOU SEE-**
I FOUND SOMEONE WHO **TRULY LOVES ME.**

BUT, **FIRST, YOU SEE-**
I HAD TO **LOVE BLESSED ME.**

FOR, ALMIGHTY **GOD, YOU SEE-**
TOLD ME THINGS THAT MADE ME LOVE THE **DAUGHTER (BARBARA) OF GOD ALMIGHTY.**

I WAS TOLD-
BY THE GOD WHO IS MORE VALUABLE THAN **EVERY POT OF GOLD-**
THAT ONE SHOULD GIVE VALUE TO ONE'S SELF, AS THE **ON LOOKERS BEHOLD.**

<u>**THE LORD JESUS SPEAKING TO BARBARA TODAY**</u>

DEAR BARBARA:
OH MY **PRECIOUS DAUGHTER.**

YOU HAVE **REACHED, YOU SEE-**

THE REALM THAT IS ABOUT TO **RELEASE ME.**

FOR, I, THE LORD **JESUS, YOU SEE-**
LOVES THE DAUGHTER WHO WAS **GIVEN TO ME.**

MY LOVE FOR YOU IS **EVERLASTING AND UNIQUE.**
IT IS A LOVE THAT EVERY **WOMAN AND MAN SEEK.**

IT IS A LOVE THAT **IS DIVINE.**
IT IS A LOVE THAT IS **YOURS AND MINE.**

IT IS A LOVE THAT IS **HOLY AND PURE-**
IT IS A LOVE THAT UNLOCKS EVERY **VALUABLE CLOSED DOOR.**

IT IS A LOVE THAT CAME FROM GOD, OUR FATHER'S, MIGHTY **HEAVENLY THRONE-**
IT IS A LOVE THAT WILL **NEVER LEAVE YOU ALONE.**

IT IS A LOVE THAT IS SURELY **YOURS AND MINE-**
IT IS A LOVE THAT HAS TRAVELED THROUGH THE REALM OF **UNINTERRUPTED SPIRITUAL TIME.**

IT IS A LOVE THAT **TRULY EXISTS-**
IT IS A FLOWING ROYAL LOVE THAT MOVES IN **EARTH'S RESIDENTS MIDST.**

IT IS **A HOLY LOVE-**

The Royal Union

FOR, IT DESCENDED TO YOU FROM **SWEET HEAVEN ABOVE.**

DEAR **BARBARA-**
O WORTHY **WELL-LOVED DAUGHTER.**

I AM YOUR ONE AND **ONLY FIRST LOVE-**
FOR, I DO SURROUND YOU WITH **THE SPIRIT OF MY HOLY DOVE.**

DEAR **BARBARA-**
DEAR FAITHFUL **DAUGHTER-**

TRUST ME. TRUST ME. **TRUST ME, DEAR BARBARA-**
FOR, I AM YOUR HEAVEN DESCENDED GIFT FROM **ALMIGHTY GOD, OUR FATHER.**

YOU DO HAVE, **DEAR BARBARA-**
THE LOVE OF CHRIST JESUS, AND ALMIGHTY GOD, **OUR ROYAL FATHER.**

TRUST US. TRUST US.
TRUST, DEAR BARBARA, YOUR GIFT OF HEAVEN SENT DIVINE LOVE CALLED **THE ROYAL CHRIST JESUS!!!**

HOLY, HOLY, HOLY-
IS THE GIFT OF DIVINE DESCENDED LOVE OF GOD **ALMIGHTY!!!**

Barbara Ann Mary Mack

BOOK # SIXTEEN

CHAINED AND BOUND

CHAINED AND BOUND

SUBTITLE:

THE DIVINE FETTERS

BY:

BARBARA ANN MARY MACK

BEGAN: OCTOBER 29, 2024

COMPLETED: NOVEMBER 9, 2024

INTRODUCTION

DEAR GOD: THE SPIRITUAL FETTERS OF YOUR DIVINE LOVE SURROUND MY BLESSED SOUL. THE CHAINS THAT SURROUND ME OFFER DIVINE WARMTH THAT I CAN HOLD AND FEEL. MY SOUL REJOICES AS I CLING TO THE DIVINE CHAINS OF LOVE THAT HAVE CAPTURED ME THROUGH THE YEARS. MY SPIRIT LEAPS WITH JOY AS I FEEL THE GENEROSITY OF YOUR CHAINS OF LOVE. OH HOLY GOD: I PRAY THAT YOU DO NOT REMOVE THE CHAINS THAT KEEP ME WITHIN YOUR REALM OF ROYAL UNINTERRUPTED DIVINE LOVE. MY SOUL CAN TASTE THE GOODNESS THAT IS PRODUCED AND RELEASED FROM THE FETTERS THAT CONTROL AND GUIDE MY WELCOMED SOUL. I GIVE YOU CONTINUOUS PRAISE, O HOLY GOD! FOR YOU HAVE WELCOMED THE VULNERABLE SOUL THAT WAS CAPTIVATED BY YOUR REALM OF SWEET DIVINITY YEARS AGO. MY WORTHY SPIRIT BOWS IN YOUR ROYAL PRESENCE, AS YOUR FETTERS CLING TO MY REALM OF GRATITUDE AND PRAISE.

ALLELUIA!!! ALLELUIA!!! ALLELUIA!!!

OH, THE WARMTH OF THE DIVINE CHAINS COMFORTS MY SATISFIED SOUL DAILY

BARBARA SPEAKING ALMIGHTY GOD

MY HEAVENLY **GOD AND FATHER-**
PLEASE LISTEN TO THE WORDS THAT COME FROM THE SOUL OF **YOUR GRATEFUL MESSENGER AND DAUGHTER.**

FOR, I AM **CHAINED TO A DIVINE LOVE-**
THAT WAS RELEASED FROM **SWEET HEAVEN ABOVE.**

I AM BOUND-
TO A HEAVEN DESCENDED LOVE AND PRESENCE THAT **ARE ALWAYS AROUND.**

I CAN SEE THE **HEAVEN SENT FETTERS-**
THAT BIND ONE OF **YOUR EARTHLY DAUGHTERS.**

OH, WHAT **JOY THAT I FEEL-**
TO BE CHAINED AND BOUND BY A ROYAL HEAVEN SENT LOVE THAT **IS EVERLASTING AND REAL.**

THE FETTERS. THE FETTERS. **THE HEAVEN SENT FETTERS-**
GRACEFULLY SECURE ONE OF YOUR EARTHLY **DAUGHTERS AND MESSENGERS.**

FOR, I, **OBEDIENTLY-**
ENJOY THE BIND AND COMMITMENT THAT **I HAVE TO THEE.**

HOLY, HOLY, HOLY-
IS MY ATTACHMENT TO GOD ALMIGHTY!!!

MY MIND, BODY, AND **SOUL, YOU SEE-**
ARE CHAINED TO THE ROYAL GOD WHO **CREATED BLESSED ME.**

FOR, **HOLY, YOU SEE-**
ARE THE HEAVEN SENT CHAINS THAT **SURROUND BLESSED ME.**

FOR, MY MIND, BODY, AND **SOUL, YOU SEE-**
DEFINITELY BELONG TO **GOD ALMIGHTY.**

FOR, **HOLY AND TRUE-**
ARE THE CHAINS THAT WERE **PRODUCED BY LOVING YOU.**

I AM WEAK FOR YOU, **MY HOLY GOD.**

Barbara Ann Mary Mack

AND, I GLADLY, REJOICE IN THE MIDST OF **YOUR DIVINE CHAINS OF LOVE.**

FOR, **HOLY AND TRUE-**
ARE THE CHAINS THAT WERE CALLED INTO EXISTENCE BY **BLESSED AND BELOVED YOU.**

HOLY, HOLY, HOLY-
ARE THE LIVING CHAINS OF LOVE THAT WERE CALLED INTO EXISTENCE BY GOD ALMIGHTY!!!

I'M CHAINED TO A DIVINE LOVE THAT IS **ETERNAL AND EVERLASTING-**
FOR, THE UNION THAT I HAVE IS WITH **CHRIST, THE FOREVER-LIVING KING.**

HE IS **HOLY AND GRACIOUS-**
AND, HE GOES BY THE GIVEN NAME OF **ALMIGHTY CHRIST JESUS.**

OURS IS AN **INSEPARABLE UNION-**
THAT CAN BE OBSERVED BY **EVERY BLESSED NATION.**

FOR, HOLY IS **THE ROYAL BEING-**
ETERNAL IS THE LIVING ESSENCE OF CHRIST, THE FOREVER-REIGNING **GOD AND KING.**

The Royal Union

DO NOT LOSE THE CHAINS **THAT BIND ME.**
FOR, THEY ARE THE VISIBILITY OF MY TRUST AND DEVOTION TO **MY SACRED GOD ALMIGHTY.**

FOR, **HOLY, YOU SEE-**
ARE THE CHAINS THAT **COMFORT ME.**

MY MIND, BODY AND SOUL ARE **CHAINED, YOU SEE-**
TO A DIVINE LOVE THAT **SATISFIES BLESSED ME.**

FOR, THE CHAINS **EMIT THE JOY-**
THAT SHINES ON THE FACES OF THE PLAYFUL **LITTLE GIRL AND BOY.**

FOR, **HOLY AND REAL-**
ARE THE COMFORTING CHAINS THAT **I CAN TRULY FEEL.**

MY GOD: I AM YOURS UNTIL THE **END OF DIVINE TIME.**
I AM YOURS, AND YOUR HOLY SPIRIT AND **PRESENCE ARE MINE.**

YOU ARE MINE, O GREAT CREATOR AND GOD OF THE UNIVERSE AND **THE BRIGHTEST STAR.**
YOURS IS A LOVE AND EXISTENCE THAT **AREN'T VERY FAR.**

Barbara Ann Mary Mack

YOU, MY HOLY GOD, HAVE CREATED AND CALLED INTO **MANIFESTED EXISTENCE-**
EVERYTHING THAT WAS DEEMED GOOD AND HOLY IN **YOUR ROYAL PRESENCE.**

BEING IN THE MIDST OF YOUR HOLINESS IS A **TRIUMPHANT EXPERIENCE-**
FOR, YOU ARE THE DIVINE REALM OF AN **UNCHAINED PRESENCE.**

FOR, YOU, O HOLY GOD, HAVE **TRIUMPHED, YOU SEE-**
OVER THE REALM OF DESTRUCTION THAT ONCE CAPTURED **MY EARTHLY LOVED ONES AND ME.**

YOURS IS A LOVE AND DEVOTION THAT **I CAN SEE AND FEEL.**
YOURS IS A LOVE THAT IS **ETERNAL AND REAL.**

HOLY IS YOUR **POWERFUL NAME-**
EVERLASTING IS YOUR **REALM OF SPIRITUAL FAME.**

EXISTENCE-
DEFINES **YOUR HOLY PRESENCE.**

FOR, **HOLY AND TRUE-**
ARE THE GREAT AND POWERFUL THINGS THAT YOU DO.

The Royal Union

I WILL REJOICE, AS I ENTER YOUR **LAND OF THE LIVING-**
AND, I WILL SING AND SHOUT HALLELUJAH, AS I OFFER TO YOU, **MY THANKS GIVING.**

FOR, **HOLY, YOU SEE-**
IS MY GRATITUDE FOR **LOVING BLESSED ME.**

AT THE DAWN OF **THE NEW DAY-**
MY HEART, SOUL, AND BODY **WILL CONSTANTLY PRAY.**

FOR, MY **PRAYERS, YOU SEE-**
ARE PRAISES TO **MY LOVELY GOD ALMIGHTY.**

HOLY, HOLY, HOLY-
ARE MY PRAYERS OF PRAISE TO CHRIST JESUS, THE ALMIGHTY!!!

VICTORY, SWEET VICTORY, HAS ENTERED THE SACRED REALM THAT MY BLESSED SPIRIT AND SOUL **SHARE WITH GOD ALMIGHTY.**

VICTORY OVER THE REALM OF **PAIN AND SUFFERING-**
HAS PRESENTED ITSELF WITHIN THE PRESENCE OF **CHRIST JESUS, THE FOREVER-REIGNING GOD AND KING.**

FOR, CHRIST JESUS, **THE ETERNAL ROYAL SON-**
HAS PRESENTED HIMSELF, AS THE EVERLASTING
GOD AND HOLY ONE.

FOR, **HOLY, YOU SEE-**
IS GOD'S REALM OF **SWEET REALITY.**

HOLY, HOLY, HOLY-
IS THE REALM OF SWEET REALITY!!!

FOR, MY GOD IS REAL; **CAN YOU NOT SEE?**
FOR, HE SHINES THROUGH **BLESSED SANCTIFIED ME.**

The Royal Union

BOOK # SEVENTEEN

CLOSER TO ME

CLOSER TO ME

BY:

BARBARA ANN MARY MACK

BEGAN: OCTOBER 29, 2024

COMPLETED: NOVEMBER 10, 2024

CLOSER AND CLOSER TO THE REALM OF ENLIGHTENMENT THAT PROCEEDS FROM THE REALM OF SWEET ETERNITY

<u>**ALMIGHTY GOD; CHRIST JESUS, SPEAKING TO EARTH'S RESIDENTS TODAY**</u>

MOVE CLOSER TO ME, **O BLESSED CHILDREN**-
SO THAT I MAY SEE THE TEARS OF JOY ON THE FACES OF **MY GREATEST CREATION.**

COME CLOSER; **COME CLOSER**-
SO THAT YOU MAY GET A GLIMPSE OF ALMIGHTY GOD, **YOUR HEAVENLY FATHER.**

COME CLOSER TO ME-
SO THAT YOU MAY FEEL THE DIVINE PRESENCE OF ALMIGHTY GOD, **THE BLESSED TRINITY.**

FOR, **I, THE LORD JESUS**-
WANT TO BEHOLD THE FACES **OF THE RIGHTEOUS.**

FOR, **HOLY, YOU SEE-**
IS THE GOD WHO CREATED THE CHILDREN WHO **BELONG TO ME.**

CLOSER AND CLOSER-
TO THE LOVE OF ALMIGHTY GOD, YOUR HEAVENLY **LIFE-SAVING FATHER.**

DEAR CHILDREN: MOVED **TOWARDS ME-**
FOR, **I AM HE-**
WHO SAVES THE CHILDREN WHO **BELONG TO ME.**

I AM THE **LIFE GIVING FATHER-**
WHO SAVES MY REPENTANT **SON AND DAUGHTER.**

I AM THE **HOLY ETERNAL ONE-**
WHO GIVES JOY TO MY **OBEDIENT DAUGHTER AND SON.**

COME CLOSER **TO ME TODAY-**
SO THAT I MAY GUIDE YOUR TRUSTING SOULS TO **MY HOLY WAY.**

FOR, **FAITHFUL, YOU SEE-**
IS YOUR HEAVENLY **GOD ALMIGHTY.**

CLOSER, CLOSER, CLOSER TO ALMIGHTY GOD, YOUR HEAVENLY **CREATOR AND FATHER.**

FOR, A LIFE **WITH ME-**
WILL OPEN YOUR HEARTS TO MY REALM OF PEACE
AND DIVINE BEAUTY.

HOLY, HOLY, HOLY-
IS THE REALM OF EVERLASTING LIFE CALLED GOD
ALMIGHTY!!!

FOR, I **MOVE, YOU SEE-**
IN THE BLESSED MIDST OF THE LOVED ONES WHO
BELONG TO ME.

HOLY, HOLY, HOLY-
IS THE REALM CALLED CHRIST JESUS, THE
ALMIGHTY!!!

BOOK # EIGHTEEN

A LIFE TIME WITH YOU

A LIFE TIME WITH YOU

SUBTITLE:

MY ROYAL GOD

BY:

BARBARA ANN MARY MACK

BEGAN: OCTOBER 29, 2024

COMPLETED: NOVEMBER 10, 2024

INTRODUCTION

A LIFE TIME OF PURE DIVINE LOVE

<u>BARBARA SPEAKING</u>

IN THE MIDST OF SWEET EXISTENCE-
MY BLESSED SPIRIT IS WITHIN ALMIGHTY GOD'S HOLY PRESENCE.

MY BLESSED SOUL IS ENVELOPED WITHIN-
YES! MY BLESSED SOUL IS SURROUNDED BY THE UNENDING LOVE OF CHRIST JESUS, MY LIFE TIME GOD AND SPIRITUAL ROYAL FRIEND.

<u>BARBARA SPEAKING TO THE ROYAL AND DIVINE CHRIST JESUS</u>

FOR, HOLY AND TRUE-
IS THE SPIRITUAL LIFE THAT I HAVE WITH YOU.

TO LIVE, AND TO LOVE-
IS A DIVINE GIFT THAT DESCENDED TO ME FROM SWEET HEAVEN ABOVE.

FOR, HOLY AND TRUE-

IS A LIFE THAT I SHARE WITH YOUR HOLY ANGELS AND YOU.

I GIVE YOU PRAISE FOR ALL OF THE WONDERFUL THINGS THAT YOU DO-
FOR, BEING WITH YOU, LORD JESUS, IS THE LIFE TIME OF LOVE THAT I WILL SPEND WITH HE WHO IS ROYAL, HOLY, AND TRUE.

HOLY, HOLY, HOLY-
IS THE ROYAL EXISTENCE OF CHRIST JESUS, THE ALMIGHTY!!!

INTO THE REALM OF SWEET EXISTENCE, MY BLESSED SPIRIT WILL SOAR-
FOR, MY LONELY YEARS ARE NO MORE.

A LIFE TIME WITH THE ALMIGHTY-
GIVES GREAT HOPE TO THE LONELY ONES AND ME.

FOR, HOLY AND TRUE-
IS MY LIFE TIME OF HAPPINESS AND JOY THAT I WILL SHARE WITH YOU.

HOLY, HOLY, HOLY-
IS THE HAPPINESS THAT I SHARE WITH CHRIST JESUS, THE ALMIGHTY!!!

A GENUINE LOVE

BARBARA SPEAKING TO THE LORD JESUS

LORD JESUS: OURS IS A GENUINE LOVE THAT **DOES EXIST.**
IT IS A DIVINE LOVE THAT WALKS IN **THE BLESSED ONES MIDST.**

IT IS A LOVE THAT TRANSCENDS **HUMAN UNDERSTANDING.**
IT IS A LOVE THAT CAME FROM THE MIGHTY THRONE OF **CHRIST, THE FOREVER REIGNING KING.**

IT IS AN **ALL-POWERFUL LOVE-**
FOR, IT EXITED THE HOLY GATES OF **SWEET HEAVEN ABOVE.**

OH, **HOW GRAND-**
TO EXPERIENCE A DIVINE LOVE THAT WAS FORMED BY THE UNLIMITED POWER OF **CHRIST JESUS' HOLY ROYAL HAND.**

I WILL MOVE IN THE MIDST OF **THIS LOVE-**

FOR, IT SURROUNDS THE HOLY ESSENCE OF THE MIGHTY KING **WHO DESCENDED TO US FROM SWEET HEAVEN ABOVE.**

IT IS UNIQUE-
IT IS A LOVE THAT THE BELIEVING ONES WOULD LIKE TO **TREASURE AND KEEP.**

IT IS A LOVE THAT GOES BEYOND; AND **WILL FOREVER LAST.**
IT IS A LOVE THAT HAS VISITED THE **PHYSICAL AND SPIRITUAL PAST.**

FOR, IT IS A LOVE THAT IS **DIVINE AND REAL.**
IT IS A LOVE THAT PIERCED THE REALM OF TIME, FOR, **NO ONE COULD STEAL.**

IT CANNOT **BE STOLEN-**
FOR, IT IS A LOVE FOR THE SAVED ONES **AND THE CHOSEN.**

HALLELUJAH! HALLELUJAH! HALLELUJAH!!!
FOR, THIS LOVE SITS ON THE MIGHTY THRONE NEXT TO **GOD, THE FATHER, JEHOVAH!!!**

FOR, **HOLY, YOU SEE-**
IS THE LOVE THAT WAS CALLED INTO EXISTENCE BY **GOD, THE FATHER, ALMIGHTY.**

HOLY, HOLY, HOLY-
IS THE LOVE THAT TRAVELED THROUGH THE REALM OF TIME WITH JEHOVAH GOD ALMIGHTY!!!

ENJOY THE SIGHT OF THIS **UNIFIED LOVE-**
FOR, IT TRULY ENTERS AND EXITS THE GATES OF **SWEET HEAVEN ABOVE.**

HOLY, HOLY, HOLY-
IS THE UNIQUENESS OF THE LOVE THAT I SHARE WITH CHRIST JESUS, THE ONLY BEGOTTEN SON OF JEHOVAH GOD ALMIGHTY!!!

OUR LOVE IS SOOTHING LIKE THE MELLOWED **OCEAN WAVES.**
OUR LOVE IS A UNION OF GREAT BLESSING, FOR I AM UNITED WITH **THE LOVE (CHRIST JESUS) THAT SAVES.**

FOR, CHRIST **JESUS, OUR HOLY SAVIOR-**
HAS UNITED WITH BARBARA, HIS **DEVOTED MESSENGER.**

HOLY, HOLY, HOLY-
IS THE LOVE OF OUR GOD AND SAVIOR; CHRIST ALMIGHTY!!!

MY GOD-

MY HEAVEN SENT REALM OF **PURE DIVINE LOVE.**

THE REALM OF **FOREVER AND EVER-**
HAS CAPTURED THE ROYAL BEINGS OF BARBARA, AND CHRIST JESUS, OUR FOREVER **REIGNING GOD AND SAVIOR.**

THE REALM OF FOREVER AND EVER **WANTS ALL TO KNOW-**
THAT I WILL WALK WITH MY ROYAL KING AND GOD WHEREVER **HIS HOLY SPIRIT AND PRESENCE GO.**

I WILL SOAR ABOVE THE HIGHEST MOUNTAIN IN THE MIDST OF **EARTH'S NEEDY RESIDENCE-**
SO THAT I MAY REMAIN IN **GOD'S HOLY PRESENCE.**

FOR, **HOLY, YOU SEE-**
IS THE ROYAL KING AND **GOD ALMIGHTY.**

HOLY, HOLY, HOLY-
IS MY LOVE FOR THE ROYAL KING, CHRIST JESUS; GOD ALMIGHTY!!!

Barbara Ann Mary Mack

SOME OF MY OTHER GOD INSPIRED PUBLISHED BOOKS

1. WORDS OF INSPIRATION
2. FATHER, ARE YOU CALLING ME? (CHILDREN'S BOOK)
3. DAUGHTER OF COURAGE
4. A HOUSE DIVIDED CANNOT STAND
5. TASTE AND SEE THE GOODNESS OF THE LORD
6. HUMILITY- THE COST OF DISCIPLESHIP
7. WILL YOU BE MY BRIDE FIRST?
8. ODE TO MY BELOVED
9. FATHER, THEY KNOW NOT WHAT THEY DO
10. IN MY FATHER'S HOUSE (CHILDREN'S BOOK)
11. IN MY GARDEN (CHILDREN'S BOOK)
12. THE BATTLE IS OVER
13. THE GOSPEL ACCORDING TO THE LAMB'S BRIDE
14. THE PRESENT TESTAMENT
15. THE PRESENT TESTAMENT VOL. 2
16. THE PRESENT TESTAMENT VOL. 3
17. THE PRESENT TESTAMENT VOL. 4
18. THE PRESENT TESTAMENT VOL. 5
19. THE PRESENT TESTAMENT VOL. 6
20. THE PRESENT TESTAMENT VOL. 7

21. THE PRESENT TESTAMENT VOL. 8
22. THE PRESENT TESTAMENT VOL. 9
23. THE PRESENT TESTAMENT VOL. 10
24. THE PRESENT TESTAMENT VOL. 11
25. THE PRESENT TESTAMENT VOL. 12
26. THE PRESENT TESTAMENT VOL. 13
27. THE PRESENT TESTAMENT VOL. 14
28. THE PRESENT TESTAMENT VOL. 15
29. THE PRESENT TESTAMENT VOL. 16
30. THE PRESENT TESTAMENT VOL. 17
31. BEHOLD THE PRESENT TESTAMENT "VOLUMES 18, 19, 20, 21, 22 AND 23"
32. BEHOLD MY PRESENT TESTAMENT "VOLUMES 24 AND 25"
33. BEHOLD MY PRESENT TESTAMENT "VOLUMES 26, 27, 28 AND 29"
34. BEHOLD MY PRESENT TESTAMENT "VOLUMES 30, 31 AND 32"
35. BEHOLD MY PRESENT TESTAMENT "VOLUMES 33 AND 34"
36. BEHOLD MY PRESENT TESTAMENT "VOLUMES 35, 36 AND 37"
37. BEHOLD MY PRESENT TESTAMENT "VOLUMES 38 & 39"
38. BEHOLD MY PRESENT TESTAMENT "VOLUMES 40 & 41"

39. BEHOLD MY PRESENT TESTAMENT "VOLUMES 42 & 43"
40. BEHOLD MY PRESENT TESTAMENT "VOLUMES 44 & 45"
41. BEHOLD MY PRESENT TESTAMENT "VOLUME 46"
42. BEHOLD MY PRESENT TESTAMENT "VOLUMES 47 & 48"
43. BEHOLD MY PRESENT TESTAMENT "VOLUMES 49 & 50"
44. BEHOLD MY PRESENT TESTAMENT "VOLUME 51"
45. LET THERE BE LOVE—CHILDREN'S BOOK
46. BEHOLD MY PRESENT TESTAMENT: "A NEW BIRTH - VOLUMES 52-56"
47. BEHOLD MY PRESENT TESTAMENT, VOLUME 57 JESUS: KING OF PEACE
48. BEHOLD MY PRESENT TESTAMENT, VOLUME 58 AND 59 "TO BE SURROUNDED BY ALMIGHTY GOD, THE BLESSED AND HOLY TRINITY" AND "I AM REDEEMED: BOUGHT WITH A PRICE"
49. HASHEM/JEHOVAH/YAHWEH: ALMIGHTY GOD, THE FATHER
50. I EXIST, SAYS ALMIGHTY GOD
51. THE KING AND I
52. YOUR DEVOTION, O LORD GOD
53. CHILD OF LOVE

54. BEHOLD THE GOD WITHIN ME: BEHOLD THE LORD JESUS
55. FOREVER AND EVER
56. I HAVE SEEN HIM
57. ALMIGHTY GOD: EXISTENCE; THE REALM OF SWEET REALITY
58. DIVINE BEAUTY: ALMIGHTY GOD
59. A TRUE SERVANT AND FRIEND OF THE LORD JESUS
60. THROUGH THE YEARS
61. CHRIST JESUS: GOD, THE FATHER'S, GREATEST DIVINE MYSTERY
62. THE DIVINE MANIFESTATION
63. A REAL LOVE
64. AND I WAS TOLD THAT CHRIST JESUS IS GOD ALSO